# REJUVENATION AND UNVEILED HIDDEN PHENIX

### Carlos Castaneda Shamanism Plus a after His Death

*Hiroyuki Nishigaki*

Writers Club Press
San Jose  New York  Lincoln  Shanghai

**Rejuvenation and Unveiled Hidden Phenix**
Carlos Castaneda Shamanism Plus a after His Death

All Rights Reserved © 2000 by Hiroyuki Nishigaki

Published by Writers Club Press
an imprint of iUniverse.com, Inc.

For information address:
iUniverse.com, Inc.
620 North 48th Street
Suite 201
Lincoln, NE  68504-3467
www.iuniverse.com

What I have written in this book is only my thought and view. Please, take
advantage of them at your peril. To avoid the risk of injury, consult your physician
and professional before beginning this or any psychic or physical exercise. The
Author and Publisher of this book disclaim any liability or loss in connection with
the exercises described and with the instructions presented herein.

ISBN: 0-595-00133-5

Printed in the United States of America

For don Juan Matus-the late Mr. Carlos Castaneda, the death defier, nagual Julian Osario, don Genaro, Buddha, the late Mr. Muriel Doreal, Thoth, kind people, the earth, inorganic allies and the spirits who have led me to the universe, the unknown world and a man of knowledge further.

# *Introduction*

I think Mr. Carlos Castaneda accomplished the feat to introduce the ancient Inca-knowledge (how to move our assemblage points-our consciousness' cores freely, how to become healthy-happy-efficient, how to bring up our immaterial fibers or third attention, the hidden supernatural power of human being, how to beckon the spirit, how to become a psychic astronaut, and how to fuse with the universe without losing consciousness and live there for 2 billion years? as an inorganic being-phenix). He sent another new bible to the world.

By the grace of Mr. Carlos Castaneda's 12 books, I can have understood the secrets of Ancient Egyptian Pyramid Text, of Cabala, of the Emerald-Tablets of Thoth-The-Atlantean, of Yoga Sutra for the first time. I think these secrets have been left behind to mankind as the legacies by those who could fly into the interior of the universe freely using their energy bodies, and can live there as a inorganic being for about 2 billion years without losing their consciousness or being killed (can live in the universe like a phenix).

When I read Mr. Carlos Castaneda's books, I was much disappointed that I felt I would not be able to write better book than Mr. Carlos Castaneda's 12 books in future. I had written 4 books about the unknown world by 1993 in Japan. Since 1993, I have stopped writing another book, and have been studying Mr. Carlos Castaneda's books. The world of Mr. Carlos Castaneda's books is so weird, stupendous, awesome, mysterious, unfathomable, exorbitant, immense, and inexplicable that I was sometimes completely lost, nearly drowned, imprisoned, nearly bitten off, or nearly killed. Sometimes, I wondered why many Americans have read such books. Sometimes, I thought many Americans and I may be foolish to read and be interested in such books, too.

Fortunately, I have recently almost passed through, swum across, flown through the world of Mr.Carlos Castaneda's books. So, I have begun to write 6 reviews about Mr.Carlos Castaneda's 12 books in my homepages since June in 1999. Then, I have rewritten them and gathered together most of them for a book. When I begun to read his books 7 years ago, I had no confidence to write in more detail than his books at all. Reviewing his books, I think now I can have added my different messages to his books. It takes me 6 years to multiply the contents of his books by about 30%.

In conclusion, the beautiful, glossy, pure, not-sticky, dry, cool light (fire) in abdomen, to beckon the spirit, to make friends with ally, to stop breath automatically, to sleep without losing consciousness or being tired in the morning, not-sticky cool sweet third attention, to absorb the peculiar feeling of strong beautiful inorganic energy (of stones, stars, the earth, allies, the spirits, the far distant universe), the space travel of energy body, to sniff-see-listen to-touch such a peculiar happy lucky feeling (light spring breeze, cunning, beauty, growing, activeness, ruthlessness, hotness, fire, sexy, abandon, confidence, largesse, joy, humor, smooth, clarity, transparence, peace, sweetness, invasion, change, sudden big collapse, hidden phenix, sadness, kindness, coolness, fog, sobriety, ripe, crazy and genius, swiftness, fierceness, bravery, rushing headlong, condense, immovability, originality, detachment, patience, coldness, water) are "emancipation", "how to become phenix", "How to become another astronaut", "the keys to open the gate of the unknown, of infinity, of another world, and of the universe". Such a peculiar happy lucky feeling can not be explained by the words of human being.

Mr. Carlos Castaneda's 12 books are almost enough. But, they do not seem to make a point of stopping your breath automatically, sleeping without losing consciousness, circulating your second attention in your physical body, burning the fire from within concretely, cleaning up your central energy pipe, making the beautiful strong energetic core of abdomen, flexible and firm abdomen, good spine, the secret of physiognomy, good complexion, rejuvenation, fasting, influence of other people and of devils, cutting the pipe of floating devil above your head, good relationship with opposite sex, dependable self-importance, good repentance, imagining powerful men such as Christ or absorbing the power of various voices and of various flights. So, I have added them. The associated press LOS ANGELES reported that Mr. Carlos Castaneda died of liver cancer at the age of 72 (?) in 1998. I think Mr. Carlos Castaneda would have never died of liver cancer if he had practiced them. Needless to say, not smoking is essential to research the universe and another world.

In addition, I have written about my space travels as a psychic astronaut because Mr.Carlos Castaneda seemed not to be able to have ventured out to the universe so that he had not written about his space travel in his 12 books. If you want become not only healthy-happy-efficient but also another astronaut or phenix, you had better read and imagine my space travel of my book so many time that your assemblage point (like a brightened egg) can move to the interior of your body and make you fly into the universe.

If you can begin to see the aura of stone after you can see the aura of human being and of plant, you can begin to see an inorganic ally or the sprits or immaterial fiber or the third attention or phenix or your assemblage point (like a brightened egg) or the universe or another world. If you rent a house where you feel relieved or relaxed and concentrate only on your inhalation and exhalation almost all day for 3 weeks, your breath will begin to stop automatically .You may notice or see stickiness, the fever of depression, coldness and numbness in your body which have weakened you and made you a blockhead. You will feel hot within your abdomen and the fire will begin to burn within your body. You can begin to erase stickiness in your body or your aura. A big explosion may happen within your abdomen or chest or head, and your central energy pipe may begin to clean up. Then, you will be able to see the aura of human being. You may begin to see the aura of plant or the aura of stone or ally or the spirit or your assemblage point (like a brightened egg) or the universe or another world. You may sleep without losing your consciousness. Your energy body may leave your physical body and travel somewhere for the first time. You may see through something or somewhere. In addition, you will be able to feel that you can shoot out your immaterial fiber or third attention to an outside object from your body and judge-control it for the first time. You can begin to have a different new happy lucky feeling. Those are the purpose of Yoga, too.

I have concentrated only on my breath almost all day for 3 weeks 5 times since 20 years ago. Doing so only once is much effective for you to research the universe and another world than reading 1000 books. If you do not do so, I think you can not understand the universe and another world at all. If you are an American, you can do so easily when you are fired or change job or divorce. You can refresh and strengthen your body or heart and you will owe me much gratitude. You may regret " I would have done so much earlier. I am stupid. I can enjoy the best feeling in my life. I feel revived". You can enjoy the same good feeling for 1-2 weeks after 3 week-fasting, too.

I often remember some founder of some leading company in Japan. He had tried to list his company in Tokyo Stock Market for several years, but had failed because of the problem of the financial statement of his company. I sometimes met him while he was trying to do so. He had never thrown away happy lucky feeling such as light spring breeze's feeling, joy, abandon, confidence, clarity, moderate sadness, detachment, originality, patience, bravery and rushing headlong under a difficult condition for several years. He often told me about the plan to list his company accompanying such a happy lucky feeling in his eyes, voice, and behavior. He had kept on eating in moderation and having good complexion. In those days, he often seemed to have been backbitten as a stupid. He told me lively, confidently and calmly with much feeling as if he had succeeded in listing his company. He can have listed his company at last. The annual earning of his company has ranked above the top 20 for 5 years in Japan. We can realize what we imagine or plan under a difficult condition as long as we keep on having happy lucky feeling, having good complexion and telling lively, confidently and calmly with much feeling as if we succeeded. In such a case, we can shoot out our immaterial fibers or third attention to an object, judge-control it and can realize what we imagine or plan sooner or later.

It is your third attention within your body that is a phenix called God in Egypt. The third attention can be compared to a smoke in a treasure-chest or a young virgin who has a space shuttle or a missile warhead. It is very fierce and very shy. It is raised by happy lucky feeling such as light spring breeze's feeling, joy, abandon, confidence, clarity, moderate sadness, detachment, originality, patience, bravery and rushing headlong. Without accompanying such a happy lucky feeling in your eyes, voice, behavior, thought, you can not shoot out your third attention to an outside object from your body and can not judge-control it. In such a case, you can not realize what you imagine, think of, or plan. Furthermore, without such a happy lucky feeling, your third attention called phenix will hide soon and become almost dead or useless. Light spring breeze's feeling is brought up by the blue energy of strong healthy liver. Joy, abandon and confidence are brought up by the red energy of strong healthy heart. Clarity is brought up by the transparent energy of strong healthy V-spot of throat. Moderate sadness is brought up by the white energy of strong healthy lung. Detachment, originality, patience, bravery and rushing headlong are brought up by the black energy of strong healthy kidney.

Most of us have thrown away such a happy lucky feeling since most of us lost a big love, divorced or were betrayed or failed in something and so on. Most of us have become cynical or withdrawn into ourselves. Most of us weaken internal organs. Bad complexion, bad bowel movement, bad appetite, bad sleeping, bad sex, poor or flabby abdomen, stiff shoulder, rough breath, strange feeling of finger have begun to happen to most of us. As a result, our third attention hides and becomes almost dead or useless. Then, most of us become like a toothless tiger or a personal computer which is throw away into heavy oil sea, mud or sludge. Furthermore, most of us will die of cancer or heart disease sooner or later.

So, half of what I have written is how to strengthen your internal organ, how to become healthy, how to feel happier,how to have good complexion, how to get rid of poor or flabby abdomen, how to grow younger. The idea underlies my theory. If you begin to practice what I have written everyday as possible, you will begin to strengthen your internal organ, become healthy, feel happier, have good complexion and grow younger in 2-3 months. Then, beautiful glossy light (fire) will begin to twinkle in your abdomen and your third attention will begin to revive little by little. The evidence of the light (fire) within your body is to grow at least 10-20 years old younger. Don Juan Matus, the teacher of Carlos Castaneda looked younger than his son who was in his mid-sixties. I am a 59 year old

Japanese and look 10-20 years old younger. Sometimes, I look 25 years old younger.

To be able to sleep without losing consciousness and not being tired in the morning is the memorial wall for you to get over as well as to stop breath automatically. When you can burn the fire within your body practicing Part 1 of my book, you can begin to sleep without losing consciousness or being tired in the morning. While sleeping without losing consciousness, you can change your dream easily, shoot out your immaterial fiber or third attention to an object easily and realize what you imagine or think of easily. In such a case, what you image, think of, act, see, sniff, tell, hear or touch in your dream while sleeping is neither a dream nor a illusion. It is a reality. You can work both in daytime and at night. Maybe, you may work more at night than in daytime.

Strong full sex energy can get up to warm the core of abdomen within the central energy pipe of your body. Then, the fire begins to burn within the core of abdomen. At the beginning, the fire suddenly rises from the core of abdomen to swallow you so that you are swallowed by red energy and can not see besides it for a while. Since then, you can often feel and see the fire suddenly rises within your central energy pipe. It can be compared to an exercise of a chicken of phenix. When you look into your body, you see the fire is burning from within your body. As a result, you can begin to sleep without losing consciousness or being tired in the morning. To be able to sleep without losing consciousness, you had better save your sex energy as possible and finish eating before sunset. You had better strengthen your sex energy, save it and make it get up to warm the core of abdomen. In this respect, you have to grow younger as possible.

About a week ago at night, I saw my TV which broadcasted about 40 old people who have come back to their village near Chernoby in Ukraina on television. The area around Chernoby has been off-limits because the big atomic accident happened to the atomic power plant in Chernoby. They seemed to want to live in the good old village as an agriculturist, want to die there and want to be buried there because they are old. I saw they ate the agricultural produces which they grew themselves on the rich soil of massive radioactivity contamination. They ate them freely. They are called the people who take many liberties by the government. One woman of them said "We differ from those who live in apartments in cities.

Human being is born from soil and returns to soil" confidently. They have helped one after another. They have taken care of the sick who lives alone and the graves of their ancestors.

At that night, I felt I slept without losing consciousness. When I remembered such old people near Chernoby in my dream, the spirit who has watched and guarded them suddenly descended to me. The spirit was transparent, green, red and yellow. It was cool and warm. Its feeling was light spring breeze's feeling, free, elastic, sad and clean. The spirit engulfed me with such a good feeling. I am apt to lack in such a good feeling if I become weak, careless or proud. So, I flew to 40 old people near Chernoby in my dream and said to them "The spirit bless you" in return. Whenever I remember old people near Chernoby and their spirit since then, I can feel relieved and relaxed. Then, I can't help sending my message "The spirit bless you" to them carrying such a message on my third attention to them all the way from Japan.

There are hundreds of ways to temper your physical body and energy body. They look like a maze. If you follow some way for 2-3 months, your complexion will not change for better and you will not grow younger. No one asks you "You look happier. You have changed. Has something good happened to you recently?". Then, you had better leave the way. When your complexion changes for better and you can grow younger, you had better follow the way. Then, many people will begin to ask you "You looks happier. You have changed. Has something good happened to you recently?" If you want emancipation and phenix, you have to keep on growing at least 10-20 years old younger by all means. In such a case, you will never die of cancer or heart disease.

You had better look for a petty tyrant who persecutes, annoys or insults you to no end in the ordinary world. When most of us meet or deal with a petty tyrant, most of us are apt to throw away happy lucky feeling soon. Then, we become irritated or unhealthy, feel worthless, get angry, hate, fall into self-pity, make our complexion worse and look older so that our third attention becomes confined to our body and almost dead or useless. Unconsciously, we make our eyes, voices, behaviors and thoughts have unhappy unlucky feeling. A strong useful ally and spirit hate such a people and never approach-help such a people. You had better practice not throwing away happy lucky feeling under a difficult condition taking advantaging of a petty tyrant. Don't throw away happy lucky feeling while meeting and dealing with a petty tyrant. You had better temper yourself by a petty tyrant.

Maybe, unhealthy-unhappy-inefficient people can not understand my book at all because they have seldom shot out their immaterial fibers or third attention and have not followed their body-responses. They ignore my book. To the contrary, founders, pioneers, big men, enterprisers, healthy-happy-efficient people can understand my book easily and agree to what I have written because they have often used their immaterial fibers or third attention unconsciously for long years and followed their body-responses (which are written in Part 5 of my book) ignoring a plausible reason. My book reminds them very much. They are apt to not to throw away happy lucky feeling easily while meeting or dealing with a petty tyrant.

But, founders, pioneers, big men, enterprisers and healthy-happy-efficient people become at a loss what to do if once they lose happy lucky feeling, can not handle their immaterial fibers or third attention and fail in succession. They do not know how to revive their immaterial fibers or third attention. A strong reaction happens to them from losing good self-importance and self-confidence. They are at a loss as if a strong tiger suddenly become a toothless tiger. As a result, they are apt to be disgraced miserably or die of cancer or heart disease in about 3-5 years.

If you are founders, pioneers, big men, enterprisers, healthy-happy-efficient people and can become aware " I have begun to lose happy lucky feeling, be unable to handle my immaterial fiber or third attention and fail in succession " after you read my book, you had better read my book as many times as possible and practice what I have written everyday as possible for the purpose of reviving your immaterial fibers or third attention. But, I hope you will use your revived immaterial fiber or third attention to protect the environment of the earth and cherish the lives of animals, of trees and of plants as possible. It is because taking advantage of our immaterial fibers or third attention unconsciously, we are apt to destruct the environment of the earth, take-take from the earth and kill animals, trees and plants.

How to vanish physical body, fuse with the universe without losing consciousness and live there for 2 billion years? as an inorganic being (phenix)-has been written in the most detail and most concretely in Mr.

Carlos Castaneda's books. Don Juan Matus (the teacher of Mr.Carlos Castaneda), don Genaro (Mr.Carlos Castaneda's benefactorand don Juan Matus' friend) and nagual Julian Osario (the teacher of don Juan Matus) changed their physical bodies to inorganic beings, fused with the universe without losing consciousness and have lived there as an inorganic being. In the universe, the inorganic being of don Juan Matus looks like 50 years old, the inorganic being of don Genaro looks like 40 years old and the inorganic being of nagual Julian Osario looked like 60 years old (recently has suddenly looked like 35 years old). The inorganic being of the death defier looks like 35 years old. I think Christ vanished his dead body just after he was killed and has lived as an inorganic being in the universe.

But, even Buddha could not do so and was cremated 2500 years ago. Mr.Carlos Castaneda seemed to be unable to do so in 1998. He seemed to die of liver cancer and his dead body was cremated according to the associated press LOS ANGELS. I have known about such a death or life since 13 years ago. I had thought "It has no relation to me at all." 20 years ago when I was on the second floor of my house, my energy body left my physical body and looked down it for the first time and then my energy body was on the way to the universe. But, my daughter closed the door with a bang so that my energy body came back to my physical body immediately. I could have forgotten it soon. But, since I could venture out to the universe completely for the first time 3 years ago with the help of my sexy female ally, I must have recognized the possibility to die or live in such a way reluctantly and have had the complicated feeling which can not been explained by words easily.

I can not write about "How to vanish physical body, fuse with the universe without losing consciousness and live there for 2 billion years? as an inorganic being (phenix)"comfortably. I am 59 years old. I may talk to myself "I have lived enough on the surface of the earth". I think I will have to leave my family, my grand children, my mother, other people, animals, insects, plants, mountain, river, sea, rain, wind, air, snow, sunshine, moonlight and anything on the earth when I vanish my physical body, fuse with the universe without losing consciousness and live there for 2 billion years? as an inorganic being (phenix). I sometimes peep at the face of my wife who married so strange male as to think about "How to vanish physical body, fuse with the universe without losing consciousness and live there for

2 billion years? as an inorganic being (phenix)" in secret seriously. I think how my wife will think when I suddenly vanish my physical body forever and enter into the universe. Furthermore, I think sometimes I wish I had been raised by a sweet married couple and could have fallen in love with a female satisfactory in the spring of my life. Just after I think so, anything on the earth always begins to look like a jewel for me. I always begin to cherish and miss it for a few days. I am always compelled to think " I can have lived on the beautiful spaceship called the earth as a human being. Thank you".

When the earth suddenly shook and roared "Gou" violently 2 years ago, the spirit and the universe seemed to be about to take me away from the earth forever. I cried loudly "Let me stay on the earth for a while" unconsciously, then the earth stopped shaking and roaring "Gou" immediately.

If I am confined to such a feeling completely, I have to be confined to the surface of the earth, forget the feeling of the spirit, of ally, of my space travels and of the universe and can not venture out to the universe at last. In addition, if I become weak, careless or proud while being chained to such a feeling and strolling on the surface of the earth, I will have to lose my good complexion and peculiar happy lucky feeling, look older, make the light (fire) within my body go out, rot my immaterial fiber or third attention (my phenix). As a result, I will have to begin to forget the feeling of the spirit, of ally, of my space travels and of the universe so that I will have to be unable to venture out to the universe and die of cancer or heart disease and so on on the surface of the earth. That is to say, I will have to rot my phenix on the earth although I have overhauled my phenix and finished its test-flight. I will have to become stupid enough to miss the timing to cut all chains of the earth at once and the timing to become like a phenix in the universe because of my indecision. Old age called the last enemy, a new petty tyrant, dirty other people's energy and devils will always try to make me weak, careless or proud by all means because I am 59 years old.

I have become very puzzled about the super high speed of my third attention. My third attention has speeded up since my first space travel that happened 3 years ago. Now my third attention can fly to almost any star within a second or 2 seconds however far away it is from the earth. I am compelled to feel that the vast universe looks likes one room in some building for my third attention. I often wonder where I go and live in the vast universe as a inorganic being (my third attention without my physical body, phenix).

There seem to be many strong dangerous unfamiliar energies in the vast universe for me. I can only have ventured out to the universe at super high speed. I am quite a stranger to the vast universe. If I become proud, careless or weak, I may be confined to some place of the universe, be exploded or melted to death immediately at last. There are many third attentions and immaterial fibers that have been confined to some place of the universe. When I find such third attention or immaterial fiber while looking up at the sky, I emancipate it if possible. Then, I can feel much pleased and relieved. Now this is one of my secret pleasures or hobbies. If I fear many strong dangerous unfamiliar energies in the vast universe too much and hold to the surface of the earth, I will have to be attacked by old age called the last enemy, a new petty tyrant, dirty other people's energy and devils and will have to die of cancer or heart disease on the surface of the earth like a drown bird on the heavy oil sea.

It is a big challenge that I will survive many strong dangerous unfamiliar energies in the vast universe and the enemies on the surface of the earth. Challenge is only challenge. Taking advantaging of or playing with such an enemy, I have to temper myself and attain the knowledge about the universe further. I have to fight against such an enemy with ultimate abandon. I have to challenge my fate with abandon, largess and humor. Only in such a case, the spirits and inorganic allies who have been watching me will help me even though I do not ask for help to them. An old smallish virile lean woman like a female hawk seems to have been fighting against such an enemy. She has been said to be 80 or 100 years old by others, but she looks like 60 years old. Her energy body suddenly visited me to the hotel like a female hawk when I attended the Tensegrity workshops (ancient Inca-style body-exercise) in the summer of 1998 in U.S.A. Since then, her energy body has sometimes visited me all the way to Japan. My physical body has not met her physical body yet, but I think I can have a good superior since then.

I hope someone will understand what I have written and multiply the contents of what I have written. Furthermore, I hope someone will be able to become a psychic astronaut and write a book as to how to become a psychic astronaut or phenix referring to what I have written, to Mr. Carlos Castaneda's books, to Emerald-Tablets of Thoth, to Ancient Egyptian Pyramid Text, to Yoga Sutra and to Cabala. But, I think it depends on whether or not someone meets the spirit. Without the flush of meeting the spirit, someone will not do so. Without it, someone can not do what other people who have not met the spirit regard as a ridiculous story. Someone will surely meet the spirit and do so sooner or later as long as someone thirsts for the spirit and acts, sees, speaks with abandon, largess and humor. The spirit likes such a man and chooses him.

I feel much pleased even though you practice some part of what I have written only to become healthy-happy-efficient or only to grow younger at your peril. Even if you practice a little bit everyday for 10-20 years patiently, carefully, not-proudly, fearlessly, soberly, it will surely pay you well. You will begin to have good complexion, grow 10-20 years old younger, burn the fire from within, multiply the peculiar happy lucky feeling and attain supernatural power little by little. You will never die of cancer as long as you have good complexion, grow 10-20 years old younger, burn the fire from within, multiply the peculiar happy lucky feeling and attain supernatural power. Don't act as if you roved from one woman (or man) to another and married no woman(or no man) or married a bad woman(or a bad man). A little bit everyday is OK. It is the most important.

I express my acknowledgements to Mr. Akitaka Nomoto, Miss. Christine Buechel and Mr. Keiji Kinebuchi who have helped me to write or submit this book.

Your thoughts or view-Send E-mail: fwng8854@nifty.com

# Contents

# Part 1

## Swim a cross Carlos Castaneda's world

—Don Juan Matus descended to me from the universe and taught me as I sent him beautiful guitar sound from the earth

1. Abandon, largess and humor can turn on beautiful body's light which can be considered a noble offering or good pheromone to beckon the spirit, opposite sex, health, friend, money, and high position

2. Good examples are four preachers who can faint audiences and cure disease marvelously with the help of their spirits

3. Weak, sweet spirits such as those of Morris Cerullo, former President Reagan and Bush, Vice-President Albert Gore are really strong and immense

4. Joyful Rodney Browne can become much stronger if he loses weight

5. Carlos Annacondia can revive the dead and faint gangs without weapon by using his strong immaterial fibers of his abdomen

6. "We are sediment or nobody without strong immaterial fibers of our abdomen I" said don Juan Matus

7. Pastor. Steve Ryder's, former bank robber's message has big punch: "Have courage in heart!"

8. Had better study the mood of four preachers, of Ronald Reagan, of Geoge Herbert Walker Bush, and of Albert Gore to beckon the spirit; listen to their tapes 100 times, will be very rewarding.

9. How to emerge from an unfortunate vicious circle and attract the spirit for happiness

10. Practicing bowel movements 6 times and constricting the anus 100 times daily enables a 70 year old man to ejaculate 3 times in succession without drawing out and to grow 20 years old younger with a beautiful light in his abdomen

11. My deepest gratitude to don Juan Matus who taught me how to change my mood immediately and completely

12. My shy sexy female ally gave me sweetness and the ability to fly enabling me to break through the white roof in the universe during my first flight

13. Cleaning up the central energy pipe, developing a beautiful glossy dry light in the abdomen, the spirit, an ally, stopping the breath naturally, sleeping without losing consciousness, and a non-sticky, cool, sweet third attention are the keys to open the gate of the universe:

14. Practice moving within oceans and the earth like a fledgling and become used to the super high speed of your third attention before your departure for the universe

NEXT Text

1. Abandon, largess and humor can turn on beautiful body's light which can be considered a noble offering or good pheromone to beckon the spirit, opposite sex, health, friend, money and high position

Whenever we act like a coward, are stingy, of irony, talk like it, see the world in this way, then all energy bodies within and around our bodies become dirty, dark, sticky or solid, causing a fever of depression, or coldness. This attracts devils which torture us. On the other hand however, whenever we do the acts of abandon, largess, humor, speak and look at the world in this way, some part of our energy bodies starts to flash, twinkle, or shine beautifully. The spirit find such beautiful lights in our energy bodies immediately, approach us at full speed, and help us, because the spirit likes beautiful immaterial lights in our energy bodies very much.

I think that it is the same in the relationship between men and women. Whenever men act out of abandon, largess, humor, talk in this way and looks through such eyes, men twinkle beautiful immaterial lights in their energy bodies. Women then can feel something special or happy about these men and approach them although most of women can not see beautiful immaterial lights of these men. Maybe, many women would like to be loved by these men quietly.

I think, beautiful immaterial light in energy body triggered by the acts of abandon, of largess, of humor, by talking in such voices, by seeing through such eyes is a noble offering of delicious scattered food or good pheromone to beckon the spirits, opposite sex, furthermore, health, rejuvenation, longevity, happiness, joy, friends, money, high position, and so on.

How about you now? could it be that you are not satisfied with your life ? Don't hold grudge against others. One could say that you feel this way because you may have rather offered rotten fruits, meats or even your excrement. Make sure you offer noble, delicious offerings carefully to people, your body, your heart and the spirits to be able to say "I am satisfied". Be careful not to become proud. You had better keep on offering a noble delicious offering carefully to people, your body, your heart and the spirit.

2. Good examples are 4 preachers who can faint audiences and cure diseases marvelously with the help of their spirit

These good examples are Mr. Rodney. H. Browne (in Florida, U.S.A, from South Africa), Mr. Carlos Annacondia (Argentine), Mr. Morris Cerullo (Jew), Mr.Steve Ryder (Australian).They are preachers or ministers.

Four preachers can knock down, fall down, or faint their audiences for 30 seconds up to one hour without using their arms or feet. Four preachers can cure the diseases, deformities in people while they fainted, were knocked or fell down during their group sessions.

They can also change the characters of their audiences and give much joy to them. They can improve the lives of their audiences, for example in regard to financial provision. Furthermore, Mr. Carlos Annacondia and Mr. Steve Ryder said in Japan that they could revive dead persons. They have visited Japan and I have attended their events since 3 years ago. I was able to see their mysterious, powerful, and kind ability before my eyes in Japan.

They have said to their audiences that they can cure the diseases of their audiences and change the lives of their audiences only when the spirit (they have often called it God) visits them and works on their audiences through them.

To beckon the spirit, entice it, become familiar with it and express it with their acts, they act out of abandon, largess, and humor. They are bringing out the best of themselves and offer it to the spirit before their audiences begin to fall and get knocked down, or faint. I think that they are warriors, too, according to the book, the Power of Silence by Mr. Carlos Castaneda, although they are preachers or ministers. It is because they can beckon the spirit. Furthermore, it is because they can shoot out their immaterial fibers to an object (their audiences) from their abdomen and judge-control it.

The spirit is abstract, intent, and God because the spirit looks like red, white, blue, transparent or yellow fog or gas or light which has intent, emotion and silent knowledge. The spirit can immediately penetrate into anybody, anything or any place, and travel into the interior of the universe at super high speed faster than that of a light. The spirit is floating in the air, inside the earth and in the universe. It is abstract, empty, but it can immediately turn into any definite immaterial body if it wants.

I think the color of the spirit is not only of dark gold dust, but also of different colored dusts. The spirits (knowledge) are different in character, ability, color, smell, contact feeling, sound, speed and temperature one after another.

3. Weak, sweet spirits such as those of Morris Cerullo, former President Ronald Reagan, Geoge Bush, Vice-President Albert Gore are really strong and immense

The spirit becomes much stronger and nimbler in proportion to the degree of the spirit's dryness, nobleness, gloss, kindness, weakness, clearness, and sweetness. There are many strong and nimble spirits who seem to be weak on first sight. That is the same as among human beings. Strong and agile men often seem to be weak on first sight.

The spirit of Mr. Morris Cerullo, and the spirits of former US Presidents Geoge Bush and Reagan, and of US Vice-President Albert Gore, seem to be weak, sweet and kind on first sight, but they are really very strong.

The color of Mr. Morris' spirit is blue, transparent, and white. He often said "I am a Jew and an orphan. My parents died when I was 2 years old. I was raised in an orphanage". He said in June, 1998 in Japan " I preached 30 thousand Haitians and fought against 300 Haitian witches who came to my ministerial meeting and tried to kill me".

The color of Mr. Reagan's spirit is white blue. Mr. Reagan's spirit seems to be weak and sweet, but really incredibly enormous. His spirit can disarm anybody without orders or threat, and can use anybody freely without orders. Anybody is apt to follow his spirit voluntarily. Many people wondered why this third rate actor was able to elected as the President of U.S.A. Many people thought" I seem to have better head than that of Mr. Reagan's." I think that his incredible, enormous spirit loved Mr. Reagan and led to his being elected.

Similarly, the spirits of Mr. Bush, of Mr. Albert Gore are weak and sweet on first sight, but really strong and immense. The spirit of Mr. Bush is of red-orange color, has a secret weapon like a sharp dagger side-thrown by hand, and can enlarge to the same width of the state of California about 2 thousand km high. I can feel Mr. Bush has become more powerful, excellent, healthier and happier than during the presidency of U.S.A. He would become much better President than before. I can see that his son has begun to climb a beautiful tense rope upward slowly which the universe hangs since the summer of 1999. The beautiful strong spirit has begun to touch his son and make his son flash since the 1999 spring.

The spirit of Mr. Gore is of noble transparent color and has the mood of noble silent weak old woman, but has a secret weapon like a sharp needle which stabs the medulla oblongata of enemies' without their noticing it, and has a better head than computer. I think that if Mr.Gore becomes the President of U.S.A, the peculiar silence, peace, cool, sharpness, and sweetness of his spirit will govern our earth.

Although these 3 big men in the political world of U.S.A have not practiced special training for warriors, and shamans, I think they are also warriors and modern shamans because they have been much loved by their spirits. I am sure they have been of so much abandon, of so much largess, of so much humor that they have been much loved by their spirits. I think they must have been liked by many women, too.

4. Joyful Rodney Browne has the potential to become much stronger if he reduces his body weight.

Mr. Rodney. H. Browne succeeded in beckoning the spirit in 1979 in South Africa for the first time. He had been thirsting and hungering for the spirit, and been praying and crying " Give me your power!", "Fire! burn! be filled!". Then, the spirit with the character of fire suddenly descended into him, so that the living water began to overflow from the bottom of his abdomen.

Mr. Rodney. H. Browne began to laugh, cry and talk in unknown voices, and had been drunken by the spirit of fire for 3 days. He felt as if he might die. He has big white energy pipe on his back which is half a foot in diameter and 5 feet in length. He has the black red spirit who is joyful, courageous, strong, immense, sweet, of abandon, of largess, and of humor. His spirit is like a super tidal wave or a super wing-bird. I think he has much hidden ability to become a good astronaut if he wants. His spirit can overflow Japan in 2 seconds, or make a vertical take-off and landing that could be compared to an aircraft.

But, I wonder why Mr. Rodney. H. Browne does not reduce his body weight. He is too fat, which gives his voice a painful tone, and his aura and his energy body are not very dry but a little sticky (human form called by Mr. Carlos Castaneda). I believe that his being obese must be the cause of diabetes, heart disease or cerebral hemorrhage, sooner or later. I wonder why his spirit (he calls it God) has not advised him to lose much of his weight because his spirit has been advising him to succeed in the U.S.A in only 12 years.

He said that he emigrated to U.S.A with only about 300 dollars in 1987, and could not afford to buy a car for 7 months after his emigration. He is now 38 years old. By the grace of his spirit' good advises, he has succeeded in U.S.A to held his big mission-meeting at Madison square garden in New York from July 7 to August 13 in 1999.

Personal power is a lucky or happy feeling. I think Mr. Rodney. H. Browne will feel much more lucky or happier if he succeeds in reducing his body weight. Mr. Rodney. H. Browne will become much more powerful and give much more joy to more people, and save more people if he succeeds in reducing his body weight. I expect he will be able to do so or may have done so already.

5. Carlos Annacondia can revive the dead and faint gangs not by using weapon but by using strong immaterial fiber of his abdomen

Mr. Carlos Annacondia ran a screw plant in Argentine. He had about 80 employees. He had been thirsty and hungry for the spirit and prayed for the spirit. Then, the spirit descended into him. Following the voice of his spirit, he gave up his business and became a preacher. This was during Falcon Island War. He said that he knew only one story of the Scriptures at that time, so he started to preach at slums to exaggerate one story of the Scriptures to gain time. He often said "The way to open the gate of heaven (to beckon the spirit) is to forgive yourself and others". He said "One day, a young crippled women was crying "I forgive my father" in succession loudly at my meeting, then threw down a pair of her crutches, and could begin to walk without them".

When Mr. Carlos Annacondia visited Japan in 1998 September. I saw his spirit is transparent and green where a noble female angel and a plump male live. This noble female angel dislikes the plump male whose color is black and yellow. I said to this plump male "Don't worry Mr. Annacondia". Many people have stopped smoking drug where Mr. Carlos Annacondia has come and preached, so many gangs have tried to assassin him with guns or rifles. But, the gangs have failed to kill him because Mr. Carlos Annacondia made them faint during his session without using his arms or feet while the gangs held guns and riffles. This is the proof that he has a highly developed and strong immaterial fiber that shot out to the gangs from his abdomen and fainted the gangs.

Highly developed and strong immaterial fiber is a qualification of a warrior, or shaman. Furthermore, A Separate Reality says "(Inner) intent (a bunch of well-developed strong immaterial fibers) is what can make a man succeed when his thought tells him that he is defeated. (Inner) intent is what makes him invulnerable". "The biggest purpose of a warrior's or shaman's is to revive practically dead, useless (inner) intent which dose not respond voluntarily. An average man has practically dead, useless (inner) intent which dose not respond voluntarily".

6. "We are sediment or nobody without strong immaterial fibers of our abdomen I" said don Juan Matus

Don. Juan. Matus, yaqui Indian, the teacher of Mr. Carlos Castaneda said " We are sediment or nobody without inner intent (highly developed strong immaterial fibers)".They should be like those of Mr. Carlos Annacondia to shoot out to the gangs from the center of his abdomen and fainted the gangs whenever they tried to assassin Mr. Carlos Annacondia in Argentine.

Not only Mr. Carlos Annacondia but also Mr. Morris Cerullo, Mr. Rodney. H. Browne, Mr. Steve Ryder have plenty of highly developed strong immaterial fibers which shoot out from the centers of their abdomens. This makes them knock down or fall down and faint their audiences.

When Mr. Carlos Annacondia preached in September in 1998 in Japan, he seemed to be tired at first. But, he turned to be much powerful when he began to look up constantly and a barrel of nectar at the top of his head suddenly flowed down his body. He has had the most nectar among the people whom I have seen. His nectar is cool, pure, noble, and fragrant, which can cure disease, give much peace. The book, Journey to Ixtran by Mr.Carlos Castaneda says about the same kind of nectar which flowed down from the top of Mr.Carlos castaneda's head at his best power-spot place in Mexico. Such nectar can erase a personal history (bad self-importance, hate, sadness and self-pity), sticky energy body (human form), and lead man into inner silence which can beckon the spirit.

7. Preacher. Steve Ryder, former bank-robber's message has big punch: "Have courage in heart"

Mr. Steve Ryder (born in 1937) said "I was a bank robber, and sentenced to be in prison for 20 years in Australia". When he was on parole, he heard the preach of the Billy Graham Crusade that "One is saved who believes in God". He thought that I was a parolee, sentenced to be in prison for 20 years, and unhappy. He thought he would be able to believe in God if God gave him the same power as that of Christ's. He was wondering what gift would be given to him by God without eating food for 3 days. At one point, he wanted to enter into a basement room of a certain hospital in Australia. He entered into this room and the spirit, like white gas engulfed him. While he was going out this room and walking along the corridor of the hospital, the nurses he encountered fainted.

Mr. Steve Ryder said to his audiences in Japan "I was arrested for armed robbery, sentenced to be in prison for 20 years, and lives vigorously now. Please, have courage in your heart if you are of pain, illness, worry, or grieve in your life". His message had big punch, much persuasiveness and strong impression.

8. Had better study the mood of four preachers, of the former President. Reagan, Bush, Vice-President. Albert Gore to beckon the spirit; listen to their tapes 100 times

I recommend my readers to attend a meeting which Mr. Rodney. H. Browne (his church,River At Tampa-Bay in Florida in U,S,A), Mr. Carlos Annacondia, Mr.Morris Cerullo or Mr.Steve Ryder (Reach out for Christ international ministries) will hold. Watch their gestures, hear their voices, and see their eyes, so that you can understand why they can beckon the spirits. Their gestures are acts of abandon, of largess, of humor. The mood of their voices and eyes are full of abandon, of largess, of humor. Imitate their acts and the moods of their voices, of their eyes if you have not yet been loved by the spirit and you thirst for being loved by the spirit. Buy their tapes and listen to their voices at least 100 times, too.

Also observe the actions, voices and eyes of former US President Bush or Vice-President of U.S.A. Albert Gore who have the moods of abandon, largess, humor, and not forget their moods. Buy the tapes of speeches by former US President Reagan which were recorded in his greatest glory, and listen 100 times.

This will enable you to distinguish the voice which can beckon the spirit, from the voice which can not beckon the spirit, sooner or later. I think their spirits will begin to appear in front of you, begin to love you, and begin to give you some or small part of the same power.

After this, detect the voices of the nature, of the inner-earth, of the universe which can give you happiness and power, and hear their voices as many times as possible. You will be healed to remember the moods of these voices if you are tired or depressed. That is to say, you can beckon the spirit floating in the nature, the inner-earth or the universe. The Scriptures say that sheep can detect the voices of a shepherd and only follow them.

9. How to emerge from an unfortunate vicious circle and attract the spirit for happiness

For most of us, practicing abandon, largess, humor, talking in such a manner and seeing through such eyes become very difficult when our bodies are weak and unhealthy. When our bodies are weak and unhealthy, most of us have the tendency towards cowardice, stinginess, irony, also speak in such a way, and see through such eyes, no matter how persistently we want to avoid it. As a result of such acting, talking, and seeing, most of us can not attract the spirit when we need its help of the spirit the most.

Consequently, most of us will tend to be of more complaint, grudge, pain, illness, worry or grieve, of less abandon, less largess and less humor. And what's more we may start believing that there is no spirit or God. This is vicious circle.

Those who have been attracting their spirits, will not be able to beckon them once they get into this vicious circle. Their spirits will hate them and fly away from them. However once they realize that and emerge from it, they will be able to beckon their spirits again.

★ How can we emerge from this vicious circle?

If we observe that we are coward, stingy, ironical, we need to (1) strengthen our bodies and become healthier->(2) Make our bodies stronger and healthier->(3) A healthy appetite, good sleep, good bowel movement, good sex, give a good complexion and can make us look and feel younger than our age->(4) Gradually the heart becomes stronger and healthier->(5) At times, we may experience that certain parts of the bodies feel hot, cold, painful or shivering->(6) Energy begins to rise from the abdomen to the head and return back to the abdomen as it begins to erase a personal history and sticky energy (human form called by Mr.Carlos Castaneda)->(7) As the energy circulates from the abdomen to the head, it can happen that sometimes a small weak light begins to twinkle in the abdomen which begins to erase the fever of depression, so we can feel happier->(8) This also makes us less coward, stingy, ironic in our action, speech and in the way we look at the world->(9) It makes us practice abandon, largess, humor, also when speaking and in the way we look at the world->(10) This enables us to occasionally begin to shoot out fairly well-developed immaterial fibers from the center of our abdomen and start to beckon the spirit->(11) We grow at least 10-20 years younger->(12) Big explosions occur within head, chest, abdomen, or legs->(13) Central energy-pipes in our bodies are cleaned up and begin to work again->(14) At the abdomen big, pure, noble, strong, beautiful, dry, glossy light (fire) starts to develop->(15) Inner silence is felt and it is possible to sleep without losing consciousness->(16) It can happen that breath becomes very faint and sometimes stops naturally without dying->(17) The third attention, phenix, silent knowledge, voice without voice, power of silence->(18) Journey to the infinity, the unknown, the universe or another world is possible without being killed instantly->(19) It is possible to live there as an inorganic-being with consciousness for about 2 billion years(?).

10. Practicing bowel movement 6 times and constricting the anus 100 times daily enables a 70 years old man to ejaculate three times in succession without drawing out and to grow 20 years younger with a beautiful light in his abdomen

To make your body stronger and healthier, follow the life-style of long-living British people. Japanese news reported on the research on the

life-style of about 7000 long-living British citizens. The most contributing factors to their longevity, it was reported, were, to;
1. Sleep daily for 7 hours
2. Eat breakfast, lunch and dinner at regular hour
3. Eat a well-balanced nutritious breakfast
4. Don't smoke
5.Don't drink alcohol whenever you want to stop
6.Maintain the standard weight of body
7. Practice proper body-exercise twice a week (for example, I recommend daily practicing of simple 5 Tibetian exercises as described in Ancient Secret of Fountain of Youth, or the ancient Inca-style movement called Tensegrity) or walk for more than one hour everyday.

Those who practice all these 7 factors can live 10 years longer than those who follow only 6 of them. Those who follow all 7 of them can live 20 years longer than those who do not follow at all.

I also highly recommend drinking a cup of water as soon as you get up. Then, have a bowel movement for more than 5 minutes and repeat these another 5 times during the day, even without stool discharge. Twice in the morning, twice in the daytime, twice in the evening. Also practice to dent the navel 100 times in succession and to constrict anus 100 times in succession daily. These two exercises do not require special time and a special place, since they can be practiced without being noticed by others, while on the subway or in a boring meeting. I know a Japanese man who has been doing so everyday for 20 years. He is 70 years old now, but he looks like 50. His eyes sparkle. He has a good complexion, is full of vigor, happiness and joy. He never ever complains or carries a grudge under any circumstance.

When I commented to him in admiration how vigorous he was, he told me his secret that he can ejaculate 3 times in succession without drawing out even at the age of 70. When I asked him if he wasn't disliked by his wife, because he is so energetic, he replied "I drink alcohol and fall asleep in such a case". To my question if he was able to see a ball of beautiful sparkling light in his abdomen due to his youthful and vigorous condition, he replied that he can see it sometimes, but wasn't able to understand it. "Whenever I see it, I feel weird and go to bed as soon as I can" he added.

I have taught him that it is a qualification of a teacher, a Reverend or a guru. I have taught him that it is called "living water, God" in the Scriptures, "inner intent, the third attention, a power of silence, bird of wisdom, of freedom" in the Mr.Carlos Castaneda's books, "beautiful lotus coming out in mud" "lantern, emptiness, wisdom or enlightenment" in Buddhism, "emptiness or regenerated baby" in Taoism, "gold made from lead" in alchemy or "phenix" in Egypt.

A teacher, a Reverend or a guru have talked about such a light (fire) and asked for it for long years. Ironically, they seldom have such a light in their abdomens. As a result, they are apt to have bad complexion, not to grow younger, not to become vigorous. Then, they are apt to die of cancer or heart disease sooner or later. There are hundreds of ways to burn the fire from within. That is to say, there are hundreds of ways to temper your body and heart. They are like a maze. Most of us and even a teacher, a Reverend or a guru are apt to rove from one way to another and end up practicing no way (or not practicing everyday patiently, carefully, not-proudly and soberly).

According to some German doctor, three biggest causes of cancer are unhappy childhood, keeping own feelings under and suffering from the stress of complaints (against an opposite sex, son or daughter, parents, boss, money, work or post and so on) for more than 3 years. If you have not practiced a way to burn the fire from within, these causes can make the fire of your abdomen go out so that you have lost joy, become cynical. As a result, your body can not emit strong beautiful energy so that you have bad complexion, look older and have colder sticky numb part of your body. Cancer prefers only colder sticky numb part of your body and grows there.

It is much more effective to burn the fire from within that you know only 1-2 ways and keep on practicing it everyday for 10-20 years as the above mentioned old Japanese. You will never die of cancer as long as you keep on burning the fire from within so that you have good complexion, grow at least 10-20 years younger and become vigorous.

Most readers may begin to practice the same way everyday as that of the old Japanese after they read my book. But, I think most readers will stop practicing it in 2-3 months at the latest.

11. My deepest gratitude to don Juan Matus who taught me how to change my mood immediately and completely

When I read Mr. Carlos Castaneda's books, I was very disappointed to feel that I would not be able to write a better book than his in the future. I had written 4 books about the unknown world up to 1993, which are published in Japan. In 1993, I have stopped writing another book, and instead began to study his books. The world in Mr. Carlos Castaneda's books is so weird, stupendous, awesome, mysterious, unfathomable, exorbitant, immense, and inexplicable that I was sometimes completely lost, nearly drowned, imprisoned, nearly bitten off, or nearly killed. Sometimes, I wondered why many Americans have read such books. I wondered if they hit the pipe and attain the quasi-experiences of what Mr. Carlos Castaneda has written in his books. Sometimes, I got the feeling that we all must be utterly foolish to read and be interested in such books.

Fortunately, I have recently almost passed through, swum across, flown through the world of Mr.Carlos Castaneda's books'. This made me write again, starting off with remarking on his books. By the grace of such books, I was for the first time able to understand the secrets of Ancient Egyptian Pyramid Text, of Cabala, of the Emerald-Tablets of Thoth-The-Atlantean, of Yoga Sutra. I think these secrets have been left behind to mankind as the legacies by those who could fly into the interior of the universe freely using their energy bodies, where they can live there for about 2 billion years without losing their consciousness or dying.

I would like to express my deepest gratitude to Mr. Carlos Castaneda as well as to his teacher. don Juan Matus ,also to his teacher. nagual Julian Osario whose energy bodies have sometimes visited me, and to Mr.Muriel Doreal who found the ancient Emerald Tablets of Atlantis times in Mexico and translated them into English.

Don .Juan.Matus (who had melted his body and entered into the universe in front of Mr.Carlos Castaneda) descended to the earth from the solid stand just below the thick white roof in the universe when he was touched by the good sound of a guitar which I sent to him from the earth. The next morning, don. Juan. Matus appeared on earth as if he were an angry strong tiger. As soon as I thought he hated me, he immediately changed his mood that he was about to kick me to death if I was not alert. Then again he changed completely into the mood of a beautiful, peaceful, sublime sun-set in Mexico. I truly appreciated his beautiful, peaceful, sublime mood.

Most of us can not change our self-mood and the moods of others immediately. For most of us, once we fall into our own or others' bad moods, it becomes very difficult to get out of the bad moods and we remain there for too long. Don. Juan. Matus taught me how to change the self-mood and the moods of others immediately and he also showed me how to control an environment or a dream freely.

We have to be the king in a given environment or in a dream, not a slave of it. We are not leaves at the mercy of the wind.

12. My shy sexy female ally gave me sweetness and the ability to fly enabling me to break through the white roof in the universe during my first flight

I also would like to express my deepest gratitude to my female ally (referred to as an inorganic-being in Mr. Carlos Castaneda's books) who led away me far from the earth for the first time about 3 years ago, and gave me the ability which has enabled me to fly into the far-distant universe fairly freely.

When I played within the earth and went through or into her, my female ally suddenly caught me, carried me on her back, took me out of the earth and threw me into the universe. Without her, I flew and broke through the white thick roof of the universe. The feeling of breaking through it was like breaking through a thin wet leather. I enlarged and flew away like a super high-speed big heavy shot which was about one-eighth the size of England. I rushed at the vast universe.

As soon as I thought I had to research more about the solar system, I changed my mind and returned to the earth. I returned to the white thick roof in 2 seconds and from there returned to the earth in 2 seconds. I reduced my big energy body and tried to enter into my physical body. This attempt I failed due to my super high speed. Instead I went through it and through the earth, shooting out to Quebec, Canada which is opposite Japan. I slowed down my super high speed in Quebec and played there like a wind for a while realizing the possibility of living there without physical body. Then, I went to Japan and back through the inner space. After all, I returned to my physical body in Japan from Quebec through the inner space where I came from. During 2 weeks after the first flight into the universe, I felt as if I grasped a large rock in a torrent desperately not to be swept away. That is to say, for 2 weeks I grasped and hugged the earth desperately not to be flushed away into the vast universe.

Although my female ally visited me twice, shaking the ceiling of my hometown house when I was a 10 or 11 year old boy, I was so frighten that I ran away from the female ally desperately in the neighboring fields for about half an hour and had ignored her completely since then. After reading Mr. Carlos Castaneda's books several times I could understand for the first time that she is my good friend and can give useful ability to me. Then, she appeared in front of me as a long thick log about 4 feet in length. After an interval of 46 years, she was touching my left body, and we hugged each other tightly.

She is shy, modest, endurable, not-jealous, but very strong and quick when she has to behave so. Mr.Carlos Castaneda's book says that an ally such as her tricks male human beings into entering an ally's world in the universe and confines male human beings to an ally's world [ the so-called heaven which is only one world of the vast universe, can be taken as an example]at the last for long year. But, I can not suspect my female ally. Her shyness emits peculiar noble sexiness whenever I can detect good new energy somewhere and share some part of it with her. I compensate her for my 46 year hardness with doing so. She is trustworthy for me. I think it is OK with me that I may be tricked by such a girlfriend.

Although don Juan Matus taught Mr.Carlos Castaneda that an orange colored ally which comes to the earth from the far distant universe is very offensive and dangerous, I was safe when I encountered an orange colored ally in the morning two and a half years ago. I ask her "Where do you come from ?", and she replied "You have found me in spite of the difficulty to find me". Then she suddenly jumped at my chest and I dared to hug her tightly because I thought it was a rare and good chance for me to be given the strong peculiar energy of the far distant universe. Her energy is dry, not-sticky, glossy, pure, cool, nobly fierce and nimble. I can recover just by remembering this orange colored ally, when I feel depressed. The shy sexy female ally gave me the ability to fly and much sweetness, and the orange colored ally gave me courage and recklessness.

13. Cleaning up the central energy-pipe, developing a beautiful glossy dry light in the abdomen, the spirit, an ally, stopping the breath naturally, sleeping without losing consciousness, and the non-sticky cool sweet third attention are the keys to open the gate of the universe

I am a Japanese man born in 1941, raised in the northeastern district of China until age 6 and in the mountains until age 17 about 2 hours by express train from the old Japanese capital, Kyoto. I hope you understand and will excuse me, if my English is not read easily and if it sounds strange. Hopefully you will perceive my mistakes or unusual way to express myself in English as a seasoning.

If you are so crazy that you really want to enter into the world in Mr.Carlos Castaneda's book, I highly recommend you to practice the following 4 points:

1. Become a vegetarian and keep it up as much as possible. Only fresh fish is OK. Eat plenty of soybean and sea vegetable products, instead of meats, eggs, dairy products, and milk. About 5 years ago I gave this advice to a former white schoolteacher in the US who was suffering greatly from high blood pressure, about 180. One year later he expressed his appreciation for my kindness. He started to use honorific words frequently to me, because he succeeded to cure himself completely from his high blood pressure.

2. Undergo a 3 week-fasting under the supervision of a professional in this field. Remove a bucketful of hardened deposits that have stuck to the intestines throughout so many years. About 2 weeks after finishing fasting, the gunshot of your * * will surely become longer than during the time of high school and you will be able to enjoy some inner silence and experience the feeling of the most peculiar happiness for the first time. Your complexion, and behavior, your voices, your eyes all will improve.

Then you can't help regretting that you haven't done this much sooner and waited so long.

3. Reduce the frequency of ** and of # # to less than half. Better save your sex-energy as much as possible.

4. Concentrate only on every your breath for 3 weeks except for the time when eating, sleeping, going to stool, practicing one hour proper body-exercise, taking one hour stroll, where you are alone in some house at your power-spot place.

After you are concentrating only on every your exhalation and inhalation daily for 2 weeks while shutting out your surroundings, you will be able to begin to erase your personal history [hate, sadness, self-pity], the first attention, the second attention [dream attention], your sticky human form, and the fever of depression. As a result, you will begin to be led into inner silence, peculiar peace, peculiar happiness, begin to stop your breath naturally, and begin to sleep without losing your consciousness. Then, the third attention, power of silence, bird of wisdom, of freedom will unveil. At last you will begin to make a good start to the unknown, infinity, another world, the universe without being killed by them.

In conclusion, to have a beautiful, glossy, pure, not-sticky, dry, cool light (fire) in the abdomen, to beckon the spirit, to make friends with an ally, to stop breath naturally, to sleep without losing consciousness or being tired in the morning, and to have a non-sticky cool sweet third attention are the keys to open the gate of the unknown, infinity, another world, and the universe.

★ How to stop breath naturally?

(1) Rough and long breath->(2) subtle and short breath->(3) breath in the recesses of the throat->(4) air neither enters nor goes out through nose and mouth->(5) energy or the second attention [dream attention] enters and goes out through the abdomen->(6) energy or the second attention circulates naturally from the abdomen to the head->(7) small beautiful light begins to twinkle->(8) begin to erase personal history and the sticky immaterial [human form]->(9) begin to erase the fever of depression->(10) begin to feel light and fluid->(11) one big breath happens through nose and mouth suddenly the same as just before death->(12) energy or the second attention stops

circulating naturally->(13) so peculiar inner silence, peculiar power, peculiar peace, and peculiar happiness happen that they can not be described by words->(14) begin to see, hear, touch the immaterial world->(15) can sleep without losing consciousness or being tired in the morning->(16) higher energy or the third attention (noble cool glossy dry sweet energy without the sticky immaterial or the fever of depression, silent knowledge, power of silence, bird of freedom, something which can go through the jet-black world called The Eagle in Mr.Carlos Castaneda's book-The Eagle's Gift without dying, something which can fly billions of light-years away within a second) begins to appear.

14. Practice moving within the oceans and the earth like a fledgling and become used to the super high speed of your third attention before your departure

For the next exercise, play within the oceans and within the earth like a fledgling which is practicing to leave his nest. You have to become used to the super high-speed of your unveiled third attention and have to pay special caution not to become a lost child within the vast universe.

You have to equip your third attention with a controller. If you are like a spaceship without a controller, you can not return to the earth. The Mr.Carlos Castaneda's teacher, don Juan Matus said that many reckless ancient Inca warriors shot out of the earth without the destinations in the universe who did not want to return to the earth, like the Japanese storm-troop fighters called KAMIKAZE during world war 2. As for me, I would prefer to be killed or imprisoned by the unknown in the universe more than being defeated by old age and dying of cancer, of heart disease, or of high blood pressure on the earth. Sometimes, I had been tempted to follow the reckless ancient Inca warriors as a spaceship without a controller or KAMIKAZE when I remembered the ancient Inca ruins in Mexico.

To become used to the super high-speed of your third attention and handle it, I recommend you to often immerse yourself into The River Saint-Lawrence which defines the border of the U.S.A and Canada, and reaches the arm of the Atlantic Ocean, then, within a second move across under the sea of the Atlantic Ocean to England ,for example.I think the earth is too small for the third attention of the human being. Anyway I was very surprised and confused at the super high speed of my third attention when I was able to move across the Atlantic Ocean within a second during my first experience. I felt weird under the sea at the mouth of The River Saint-Lawrence when I was about to be caught into the dark cold bottom of the Atlantic Ocean. I resisted not to be caught into it for about 3 seconds, then, I was able to rush to England within a second so vigorously that I bumped against England and turned to Iceland and Greenland.

Light is too slow and useless as the transmitter that the headquarters of the vast universe use when they have to send many orders, messages, sounds, colors, smells, emotions, killer-power, or healing power to all universe. Modern astronomy and physics have only dealt with the world of light-speed. I think the third attention of human being, and the spirit has the same immaterial element as that of the transmitter which the headquarters of the vast universe use. Some day, modern astronomy and physics will begin to research the immaterial element of the third attention and of the spirits to know more about the vast universe. The sweeter they look, the faster they move or fly. In this respect, I think the spirit of the Vice-President of U.S.A, Mr. Albert.Gore's is the fastest of the previously mentioned 7 spirits. I could not help but shiver when I had a full realization of the super high speed of my third attention that is at so fast that it is mistaken to be able to stay at two different places at the same time.

If you read Carlos Castaneda's books, Ancient Egyptian Pyramid Text, Cabala, The Emerald-Tablets of Thoth-The-Atlantean or Yoga Sutra again, you can understand them easily after you read my book. I encourage you to try them once more.

If you can not believe in my book at all, you had better read my book as a fictional novel. Or, you may send E-mail to me "You are a madman, liar, stupid, blower".

May the Holy Spirit Bless You

# Part 2

## Astronaut

How to become another astronaut in space travel. If you want not to become another astronaut, you will be able to take advantage of what I have written for the purpose of growing younger, becoming healthier, instinctive, and feeling happier. If you are a woman, you will become more charming without makeup.

I feel happy if someone read, understand my book and progress the study about Carlos Castaneda books, Ancient Egyptian Pyramid text, Cabala, The Emerald-Tablet of Thoth, Yoga Sutra, and so on. I will be much pleased to be able to contribute to it at least. I would like someone who studies them to give me advice and information about them. I saw Ms. Carol Tiggs at the workshop in U.S.A in the summer of 1998. I often wonder how Mr.Carlos Castaneda's three cohorts are getting along.

1. When the late Carlos Castaneda shot out his fiber at my eyebrows
2. A moving meeting with don Juan Matus' teacher. Julian Osario
3. When my energy body could barely reach Dragon constellation in 20 minutes
4. Who is my successor? He seems like a noble fierce hawk who can reach Dragon constellation in only 2 seconds. Sent away don Genaro to Dragon constellation
5. When don Juan Matus permitted me to write about him
6. When buttock shoots out a big violent blank
7. About beating the earth as if it were a drum and seeing it as gas or fluid
8. About the omen of an astronaut that leads the earth's shiver, fluidity and big roar. Phenix is the third attention
9. Check other energy bodies not to crash

10. How the invasive route is like a thin film->vortex->energy channel->internal organ. A Jewish pastor. Morris Cerullo is like a beautiful strong fortress

11. Why saving sex energy is indispensable for you to rotate vortex [so-called dragon] and occur a big explosion

12. How cancer will happen after 3-5 year lump, stiff shoulder and peculiar feeling in your fingers

13. How it took me 5-6 hours every night for 2 years to puff out the fever of depression about my old bitter love trouble

14. Why the etiquette of the energy body should be to touch others sparingly, although there are no manners, law, or police in the psychic world

15. The dreaming attention-the second attention that is like a sewage or diarrhea can move to other people

16. Why these etiquettes should be applied to the world around you if you love it at least

17.How a noble call-sign can beckon the ship of Egyptian Pyramid Text from the universe

NEXT Text

1. When the late Carlos Castaneda shot out his fiber at my eyebrows

When, Mr.Carlos Castaneda died a week later in 1998. I was much angry at him and spiteful to him. He was standing in the dark black world lonely like being drenched by a cold scattered shower. I had tried to contact him twice in the past a few years, but I had been ignored.

I cried several times "Where is your ally? Use it against me. Shoot out your strong immaterial fiber from your abdomen if you surely have it. Use your intent against me. Shoot it at me if you have a male sexual organ". At last, Mr.Carlos Castaneda shot out his immaterial fiber from his abdomen at my face. It stuck to my eyebrows. I detached it from my eyebrows slowly, saying "You shot it at me at last".

2. A moving meeting with don Juan Matus' teacher. Julian Osario

About 3 hours later at about 8 o'clock at night when I was drinking a canned soft drink, I saw nagual Julian Osario, don Juan Matus (the teacher of Mr.Carlos Castaneda), and don Genaro (Mr.Carlos Castaneda's benefactor and don Juan Matus' friend) floating in the sky. Nagual Julian

Osario, who was the teacher of don Juan Matus, was floating between the earth and don Juan Matus and don Genaro. Don Juan Matus and don Genaro were standing on the same stand together just below the white roof of universe. This stand has been made by them. Many birds like a skylark are flying merrily, vigorously and nimbly just below the white roof of the universe. The bird lives there which can bite off many crosses made of immaterial fibers in the universe easily, too. Violent wind is blowing above the roof whose thickness is about a foot.

I was so surprised to meet nagual Julian Osario for the first time that I shouted "Oh! lewd teacher has shown up, too. He seems to be a tough antagonist in inner space". Hearing my voice, don Juan Matus and don Genaro were laughing so intensely that they were about to roll down the stand or run the stand through their feet.

Two hours later around 10 o'clock at night, only nagual Julian Osario appeared again in front of me and approached me. At that time, I was just urinating. I said "I have not finished overhauling my energy body yet", and he said "Never mind!" taping me on my left shoulder. I felt like weeping to meet him again. I said to him "I feel I have had the teacher about the psychic world for the first time. I feel as if you were my father".

★ Julian Osario is a kind, smallish old man but has a energetic defect

Don Juan Matus often said about his teacher, nagual Julian Osario "He is an assertive and ruthless person, a lewd teacher, too". But, as for me, he looked like a kind, sweet, smallish old man. Although I felt something a little cruel about him, I felt there was something that resembled the powder of dry snake's leather or of dry bark in his energy body. I thought he would surely become more powerfully, see more, and enter into the further universe more freely than his disciple, don Juan Matus and Mr.Carlos Castaneda's benefactor, don Genaro if he could get rid of it.

Presumptuously at dead of that night, I injected the transparent cool energy of far distant universe into nagual Julian Osario after his permission. He shone transparently and coolly. I wished nagual Julian Osario could have been floating in more upper universe than don Juan Matus and don Genaro because he was the teacher of don Juan Matus. Presumptuously again, I thought I was happy if I could help him to do so at least.

3. When my energy body could barely reach Dragon constellation in 20 minutes

Since 2 years ago, the tail of Dragon constellation around the star Alpha and the star K nearby Polaris has burst out many short white immaterial fibers whenever I look up at the tail of Dragon constellation. One of many short white immaterial fibers stretches along all Dragon constellation. I had wondered why? I read the book, "Keeper of Genesis" by Mr. Robert Bauval and Mr. Graham Hancock one and half a year ago. The book says "The shaft of Khufu's pyramid at Giza in Egypt pointed to the star Alpha (within the tail of Dragon constellation) in 2500 B.C". The star Alpha has been called the womb of the universe in China.

The following day at daytime after I met don Juan Matus, don Genaro and nagual Julian Osario, I traveled to the tail of Dragon constellation to research more. When I approached it, I came to a point when I could not come closer by all means. The big pure transparent energy which swallows the tail of Dragon constellation rejected me (Pyramid Texts describes the holiest place where Akhus lives. I think it is the big pure transparent energy. The big transparent energy engulfs a star or a constellation and guards it usually. The transparent energy's size is about 100 times bigger than that of a star or constellation). So, I checked my energy body. My energy body was dirty, dark, and sticky after all. I made adjustments to my energy body. My energy body became less dirty, less dark, and less sticky; nevertheless I was rejected again.

★ I thought I did not deserve to enter into the star because of my dirtiness

So, I discharged a strong immaterial fiber like a rope upward out of my energy body at the star within the tail of Dragon constellation. After shooting out the same rope several times, I finally succeeded in anchoring onto the star at last. I climbed up my strong immaterial fiber and I approached the star. It was oval and it had hundreds of small stars. Then, I tried to enter into it several times. It itself still rejected me and did keep the gate closed. I thought I did not deserve to enter into the star within the tail of Dragon constellation. I checked my energy body again. My energy body was still fairly dirty, dark, and sticky.

At last, I sent my beautiful dry glossy sweet blue energy to the star as my noble offering to it. I cried "Please, open the gate". Then, the star accepted my noble offering and permitted it to penetrate into any part of the star slowly and silently. All color of the star changed orange red to blue for a while.

4. Who is my successor? He seems like a noble fierce hawk who can reach Dragon constellation in only 2 seconds. Sent away don Genaro to Dragon constellation

When I came back to the earth, I saw a noble Brazilian boy in his higher teens who was playing a guitar. The sound of his guitar was not-sticky, cool, weak and strong, noble and fierce, lovely and fearful, sexy and sober, of abandon and alert, sweet and ruthless, peaceful and nimble, and good-smelling which can not be explained by words on the earth. The atmosphere of his guitar's sound is the same as that of the far distant universe, of the Holy Spirit, of the third attention of human being's, or of the best power-spot place on the earth. I appreciated the sound of his guitar to my heart's content.

I think the sound of the Spanish guitar master, Mr. Sergi Vincente's has some atmosphere of the far distant universe. His guitar's sound fuses together with his third attention. He is a warrior in handling his third attention. I like Mr. Sergi Vicente. I hear his guitar music-disc almost everyday. But, his sound is neither so noble nor so fierce. It is neither so sweet nor so ruthless. The sound of Brazilian has more atmosphere of the far distant universe than that of Mr. Sergi Vincente.

So, I thought of leading the sound of young Brazilian to the star within the tail of Dragon constellation. Suddenly, two beautiful pure, dry, glossy, cool, sweet, strong, yellow immaterial fibers burst out from his abdomen and forehead and fused into one fiber just in front of him. It ventured out from the earth to the star diagonally like a young noble fierce hawk following my lead. He was able to reach the star in 2 seconds whereas it took me about 20 minutes to do so the first time.

I made him touch the star and the neighboring star for 30 seconds. He was about to drop his guitar, and looked around constantly wondering what happened to him. I pretended to ignore him thinking I could finally find the young man who has the hidden ability to become my successor. By the way, since then his energy body has the ability to sometimes travel to me to Japan all the way from Brazil. I feel nagual Julian Osario has been much pleased that I have found this Brazilian youth. I think nagual Julian

Osario may also teach, and guard him. He can speak English because he went to school in U.S.A for one and half a years.

★ Carlos Castaneda's benefactor, don Genaro burst away retrogradely to Dragon constellation

Next, I thought don Juan Matus, the teacher of Mr. Carlos Castaneda would be pleased to hear the sound of the high teen Brazilian's guitar's. So, I led it to don Juan Matus who lives below the white roof of the universe and hit him with it. He gently dropped from his transparent strong solid stand into the earth. Furthermore, I tried to send away Mr. Carlos Castaneda's joyful benefactor. don Genaro, who is don Juan Matus' friend and lived in Ixtlan in Mexico before the departure to the universe, to the star within the tail of Dragon constellation. I aimed at joyful don Genaro. I shot the sound of the high teen Brazilian's guitar's at joyful don Genaro like a cannon shell. When I shot at the joyful don Genaro, he burst away from the stand just below the white roof of the universe retrogradely in the direction of the star. Since then, I had kept on worrying about don Genaro for one month every night looking up the star. I wondered if he could succeed in reaching the star within the tail of Dragon constellation safely.

5. When don Juan Matus permitted me to write about him

When I asked don Juan Matus, the teacher of Carlos Castaneda "May I write about you in my homepage?" a few times, he sent very sweet energy to me diagonally as an O.K sign.

I am quite unaccustomed to the use of a personal computer and making a home page. I wish I could make it a more attractive one. I bought my first personal computer on April 11 in 1999 here in Japan to write about Mr. Carlos Castaneda's world. That night when I was about to finish my home page and barely uploaded it to AOL Japan, don Juan Matus, nagual Julian Osario, and an old smallish virile lean woman like a female hawk were looking down at my sleeping face. I am a 59-year-old Japanese man. I have written 4 books about the unknown world in Japanese.

★ Nagual Elias was an efficient Astronaut

Nagual Elias, the teacher of nagual Julian Osario was good at space travel by using his energy body. According to The wheel of Time, nagual

Elias sometimes brought back objects that had attracted his eyes to his disciples. Ms. Florinda Matus made Mr. Carlos Castaneda sniff these objects, feel these objects with his hands. When I can enter into the far distant universe, I feel as if I broken through the layer of gold dust at super high speed. Countless stars hide behind one star. I feel about one star as if it were one grain of gold dust. It smells like an element of metal.

★ The secrets of Pyramid Text, Cabala, Emerald-Tablet and Yoga Sutra unveiled

I have written in Part 1-Swim across "Ancient Egyptian Pyramid text, Cabala, the Emerald-Tablet of Thoth-The-Atlantean, Yoga Sutra have been left behind to mankind as the legacies by those who could fly into the interior of the universe freely using their energy bodies, where they can live for about 2 billion years without losing their consciousness or being killed", " In conclusion, the beautiful, glossy, pure, not-sticky, dry, cool light in the abdomen, to beckon the spirit, to make friends with ally (inorganic-being. dreaming emissary or scouts), to stop the breath automatically, to sleep without losing consciousness or being tired in the morning, not-sticky cool sweet third attention are the keys to open the gate of the unknown, infinity, another world, and the universe". You will be able to understand Part 2-Astronaut easily after you read the previously mentioned sentence.

6. When buttock shoots out a big violent blank

If you follow Part 1-Swim across-the life-style of the long-lived British, having a bowel movement 6 times, denting navel 100 times and constricting anus 100 times everyday, living as a vegetarian as much as possible, reducing the frequency of **and of ## to less then half, you will not be able to sleep thirsting for a young beautiful woman or man almost all night at the beginning. You feel something strong is about to pierce through the center of your body.

★ Your gray hair will begin to regain their original color in 2-3 months

When you live in moderation and regularity, practicing physical exercise and saving your sex energy, something positive must happen to you sooner or later.

If you are less than 40 or 50 years old, you may become impatient and want to rape secretively. Surprisingly, you are not tired in spite of little sleep and start beginning to feel happier, and your hair will begin to grow back blond or black in 2-3 months. Hair may even start growing where on balding areas. Also your complexion changes for better and you begin to grow younger. Your eyes begin to twinkle. If you are a young woman, you will begin to be proposed by more men. If you are a wife, you will begin to be more loved by your husband than before. Others often begin to ask you "Has anything good happened to you recently?". You reply "Because I read a Japanese book, and I have tried" or you may simply smile secretively.

Gray hair of head-> white hair of face-> white hair of **-> white hair of ##-> pass away. "Where do you have gray hair on your body now?".

★ You'll be very pleased to realize to become full of energy for the first time

Within a year, some part of your body becomes painful, hot, and may shiver. Then, the root chakra between anus and sexual organ, anus, or sexual organ sometimes begins to shoot out energy violently like a big blank.

Such a big blank is much more violent than nocturnal emission, diarrhea and **. You look into your brief secretively. You brief is not wet or dirty, so you are very pleased to realize to become full of energy for the first time. That is to say, you have had strong immaterial fibers of root chakra, anus, or sexual organ which shoot out downwards or diagonally at last.

★ Supernatural power is proportionate to happy feeling

By these strong immaterial fibers, you can please the opposite sex more than before. But, you had better save your sex energy as much as possible, if you want to become an astronaut and be healthier or more instinctive, increase your supernatural power and feel much happier. The degree of your supernatural power is in proportion to the degree of your happy feeling, of your inner silence, of your good complexion, of your good bowel movement, of your health, of your instinct, of your rejuvenation, of your strength, of your sex energy, of your nimbleness, of your flexibility, of your subtle breathing, and of your energy body's beauty [dryness, cool, sweet, fluidity].

★ Happy, healthy or successful people have supernatural power and beautiful immaterial lights

Ironically, most pastors and most teachers of the psychic world are apt to have bad complexion, weakness and solidity, and look old. Their believers often have better complexion, more strength and flexibility, grow younger, and look happier than most pastors and psychic teachers.

Ironically, unhappy people, who need supernatural power to become happy or healthy, have not supernatural power at all. Happy people, who do not need supernatural power to become happier than now, have much supernatural power. In this respect, unhappy people are apt not to be able to understand my writings at all. Happy, healthy, or successful people can understand my writings easily and will agree with it.

For example, happy, healthy, or successful people are more or less dreamers [maybe seers, too] or stalkers and are good at it without special training or reading Mr. Carlos Castaneda's books. They have beautiful immaterial lights within their bodies, too. Such lights are the origins of supernatural power, of happiness, of health, of rejuvenation, of good complexion, of good bowel movement, of instinct, of subtle breath, of strength, of sex energy, of flexibility, of dreamer, of seer, and of stalker. How to turn on such a light has been written in Part 1-Swim across.

★ When your root chakra leaks sweet mucus or become an exciting womb

Besides shooting out a big blank from your buttock, you can feel as if your root chakra leaked sweet hot mucus. You can feel your root chakra as if it were an exciting womb. Cabala says " Human being could have lived on the earth of high temperature long years ago as a human being of immaterial hermaphrodite". I think there has been the imprint of immaterial hermaphrodite in our physical body.

7. About beating the earth as if it were a drum and seeing it as gas or fluid

An about 30 years old Japanese man, who has a wife, has been practicing Part 1-Swim Across as possible since January 1998. He was practicing for 3-5 hours including a daily one-hour stroll. He could spend in the winter of 1999 even in snow or outdoor with a short-sleeved although he has low blood pressure, not higher than 90.

I went skiing with him just after he completed 2 week fasting in the winter of 1999. He said he felt as if he has beaten the earth with his legs, and the white spirit engulfed him for the first time while skiing.

★ Seeing the earth as fluid is one of the sub-keys to open the gate of the universe

You will be able to beat the earth with your legs or hands as if the earth were a drum. Your strong energy shoots out into the earth and the earth begins to shiver whenever you beat the earth. When you can beat the earth, the earth looks like a gassy big ball or something fluid. Seeing the earth like a gassy big ball or something fluid is one of the sub-keys to open the gate of universe. You can not break through solids if you see them as solids. After you can see solids as gas or fluid, you can penetrate into and break through anything or any place immediately. You have to break through many stars immediately to enter into the far distant universe.

After such a phenomenon, a big explosion will begin to occur within your head, chest, abdomen, or legs. My first big explosion occurred within my head during the flight by plane over the Arctic Circle 25 years ago. When a big explosion occurred within abdomen 2 years ago, I felt dizzy and could not stand up for a while. Your abdomen may begin to shoot out a big blank upward through the top of your head, and a big vortex of your second attention (dream attention) may begin to whirl automatically within your head, chest, abdomen or legs.

When I was about 28 years old, I read a few pages about the spiritual world. The next day, I could see the mountains by the biggest lake Biwako in Japan as something gassy or fluid for the first time. About 21 years ago when I was 38 years old trying to fuse my voice into the blue, red, yellow, white, or black immaterial (the spirit) of the universe, I saw all buildings and the earth as something completely gassy or fluid in front of Tokyo station in Japan. I wondered what happened to me. So, I leaped up and beat the earth by my legs many times. Whenever I beat the earth with all my might, the earth dented and shivered.

8. About the omen of an astronaut that leads the earth's shiver, fluidity, and big roar. Phenix is the third attention of human being's

About 5 years ago, I visited the River Saint-Lawrence which defines the border of U.S.A and Canada. As soon as I reached the center of the wooden bridge over the River Saint-Lawrence, this bridge suddenly shivered violently and this torrent river roared "Gou" while whirling around.

Strangely, I was so completely excited and shivered that I was eager to enter into this torrent river by all means and entered into this torrent river ignoring the warning plate "Danger, don't enter into this torrent". I crossed the 10 feet high wire netting of the riverbank crazily, entered into this torrent, and desperately grasped the big stone of the riverbank not to be flowed away.

This was the omen that I could become an astronaut using my energy body 2 years later. So, I was so excited about the shiver, fluidity, and big roar on the bridge over the River Saint-Lawrence. Just before my departure to the universe, the earth shivers, becomes fluid, and roars. After returning to the earth from the universe, for 2 weeks I feel as if I desperately hugged a big stone in a torrent to prevent being flushed back to the universe.

The following day, just one hour before sun-set in the state of Quebec in Canada, I was engulfed by the beautiful, glossy, sweet, weak, kind, dry, noble, fierce, active, green-blue immaterial energy (the spirit). The most nectar at the top of my head was flowing down my body and made me enter into the peculiar inner silence and peculiar happiness that can not be described by words. I was burned coolly and sweetly.

★ My best power-spot is cold Quebec in Canada and I like the fresh snow twinkling in the strong sunbeam

My best power-spot place is in the state of Quebec in Canada. Modern astronomy says "Most of the universe is in absolute zero (-273.15 C')". By the way, presumably, I tend to like cold places on the earth. Whenever I saw pure fresh snow or ice twinkling in the strong winter-sun when I was in elementary school, I was excited and my abdomen became warm even though the tip of my toes were numb due to the cold. I feel very sorry that my physical body can't visit Quebec more often. Only my energy body can often visit Quebec. I have 5 small power spots in Japan. At one of these small power spots in Japan, I feel very relaxed. It has the glossy, dry, sweet, noble, black, immaterial energy. My back tends to become warm, very comfortable and I can peek into the interior of the earth easily, but I can not be so burned there as in the state of Quebec in Canada.

★ A rectangle-cube of special ratio and Phenix called God in Egypt

Before I enter into the universe, the unknown, or another world, some part of the earth looks like gas or fluid, dents, and shivers at least. Many transparent rectangle-cubes of the same type proportion as the stones of the Ancient Egyptian Pyramid often appear in front of me. In the science magazine-Scientific American, I read in an issue of the 70 ties "Rectangle-cube of special ratio, such as 300-50-30 (Noah's Ark) is something special". In the book, Urban Shaman, Mr. Serge Kahili King writes "Spinning rectangle cube of special ratio can generate energy". My warrior-dancing begins. I leap up and beat the earth with my heels with all my might many times. It is said in the acupuncture and moxibustion world that stimulating the heels strengthens the sex energy. Something strong then pierces the central energy pipe of my body.

I then can feel that the central energy pipe of my body is cleaned up and begins to work on. As a result, I can feel my not-sticky cool sweet super high-speed third attention unveils. I can feel I have finished overhauling my third attention. I think the third attention of human being's can be compared to Phenix called God in Egypt.

9. Check other energy bodies not to crash

Next, I check whether or not energy bodies of other living men or women stay or hide within my body, on the surface of my body, in front of me, or above me carefully.

★ Other energy bodies can be compared to cellular phones in jumbo jet or many birds wheeling above an airport

Other energy bodies within my body or on the surface of my body can be compared to personal computers or cellular phones used by passenger in jumbo jet taking off or landing.

If there is a passenger who does not follow the warning "Please, don't use now", jumbo jet faces the peril to fail to take off or land, resulting in a crash.

Other energy bodies in front of me or above me can be compared to the situation when many birds wheel above an airport. Jumbo jet taking off or landing inhales birds through the fan. Furthermore, crushed dead bodies of many birds soil the front window of jumbo jet, so that the vision is obstructed facing the danger to crash the jumbo jet.

★ When a hidden dirty energy body tried to touch the red star first rudely

2 years ago, I shot out my energy body from my chest to the star which has a beautiful glossy pure healthy red energy. When my energy body hit the red star, it radiated red light violently. Since then, the red star has often appeared. I could see it through the roof of my house many times. A few times at the beginning, I went out of my house, looked up at the sky, and saw the picture of the constellation. The red star shone right over my head like a noble woman as if she said "Look at me, look at me". The red star is a variable star which can be found most easily in November or December in Japan. The red star presented me with noble red energy and purified my dirty energy fairly.

At last 8 months ago, I ventured out to the red star to research in detail. Just in front of the red star, a dirty black energy body of another man, who hid in my left back shoulder and stuck there secretively, suddenly burst from me. This dirty black energy body tried to touch the noble red star rudely before I reached the red star. I regretted as if my noble lover was about to be touched by another man in front of me. So, I stopped to travel to the red star and returned to the earth immediately.

Every time before I venture out to the universe, I confirm that no energy bodies of other people stay in my body, on the surface of my body, in front of me, or above me. If I can detect other energy bodies, I stop space travel. I have to communicate with my destination in the universe before my space travel. I sniff, see, and hear my destination from the earth. It is difficult for me to sniff, see and hear my destination through other energy bodies or together with them. I can not receive the correct information from the universe. This is dangerous.

★ A woman's energy body is good at stalking and sticking to others secretively

If you reach this stage, you never want to seduce an opposite sex and so on. You like plain, modest, frank women or men and you hate obstinate, bold, immodest, sly women or men. A woman's energy body is softer than the energy body of a man. The energy body of a woman is good at stalking and sticking to another human being secretively for a long time whom she is interested in or loves. Consciously or unconsciously, she can control another human beings or absorb the precious energy of others through her energy body for a long time. In this respect,weak women are apt to be much stronger than strong men.

If you are not alert and you fail to detect such a woman's energy body in your body or around your body, you can be compared to a personal computer that has a computer virus. Although this woman's energy has healing power, you will become depressed, irritated, impotent, or unhealthy if this woman's energy body stays in or around your body for a long time. That is to say, no matter how nutritious and delicious food is, you will become bored and unhealthy if you keep on eating only the same food for a long time.

10. How the invasive route is like a thin film->vortex->energy channel->internal organ. A Jewish pastor. Morris Cerullo is like a beautiful strong fortress

The route for other dirty energy bodies of other people or for devils to enter into your heart, liver, spleen, lung, or kidney is [1] dirty, sticky, feverish, cold, solid, or numb immaterial thin film which is about a foot separate from your physical body-> [2] dirty, sticky, feverish, cold, solid, or numb vortex on the surface of your physical body-> [3] dirty, sticky, feverish, cold, solid, or numb immaterial energy channel of your weak small intestine and weak pancreas, of your weak gallbladder, of your weak stomach, of your weak large intestine or of your weak bladder->[4] {your weak small intestine or pancreas->heart}, {weak gallbladder->liver}, {weak stomach->spleen}, {weak large intestine->lung}, or {weak bladder->kidney}.

★ How to shut out other dirty energy bodies and devils

If you turn on beautiful dry, glossy, cool, sweet, fluid, active immaterial light in or around your body, you can beckon the holy spirit and permit neither other dirty energy bodies nor devils to enter into your body. How to turn on such a beautiful light in or around your body has been described in Part 1-Swim Across. The Holy Spirit can drive out dirty energy bodies or devils within about 2 seconds. Such a beautiful light in or around you can shut out dirty energy bodies or devils, too. Dirty energy bodies or devils can only enter into your dirty sticky, feverish, cold, solid, or numb body which has not such a beautiful light. A good example is a Jewish pastor, Mr. Morris Cerullo. His head and chest twinkle so beautifully and violently that they appear like a strong fortress. I hope he will live much longer. If he passes away in near future, my psychic eye will turn to be undependable and all my writing in my book will not become reality rather than a short fictional story. Or, you have to drive out other dirty energy bodies or devils with your strong secret weapon.

If you can not beckon the Holy Spirit, can not turn on such a beautiful light in or around your physical body, or can not use your strong secret weapon, you will be defeated by other rude dirty energy bodies and devils, and will be killed in 3-5 years.

Other dirty energy bodies and devils detect your weak castle gates [immaterial thin film, vortex, and energy channel] which are dirty, sticky, feverish, cold, solid, or numb, and break through your weak castle gates. The weak king, that is to say, a weak unhealthy heart, liver, spleen, lung or kidney has weak castle gates. If dirty energy bodies of others' or devils often begin to visit or live in your heart, liver, spleen, lung, or kidney, your aura around you, your vortex, the energy channel of your internal organs, and your internal organ will become more dirty, sticky, feverish, cold, solid or numb. Your energy body will seem as if it were cut by sharp sword and festered.

11. Why saving sex energy is indispensable for you to rotate vortex [so-called dragon]and occur a big explosion

Vortex has been called a dragon in China which can enter into the universe. There are two types of vortexes. Automatically, one rotates horizontally within the physical body, another rotates vertically on the surface of physical body or within physical body.

The vortex begins to rotate automatically within physical body horizontally or vertically after a big explosion occurs within the head, chest, abdomen, or legs. It begins to rotate so after the central energy pipe between the root chakra and the crown chakra begins to be cleaned up, too. I asked the previously mentioned Japanese who has been practicing Part 1-Swim Across as much as possible since January, 1998 and who became so vigorous that he could spend in the winter of 1999, even in snow or outdoors with short-sleeved "Can you begin to cure other's disease or Can a big explosion occur or Can your vortex begin to rotate automatically, because you have become so vigorous that you can spend cold this winter with half-sleeved?". He replied "None of them has happened to me". I said "Very strange. Why?", "I can understand the origin. It is because you are very intimate with your wife". He replied "I am not so intimate with my wife". I said "Much more strange. Why? Why?".

He replied "I have done ##" reluctantly. So, I said "You had better reduce the frequency of # #to less than half, and you will be able to cure other's disease and furthermore the rotation of your vortexes and a big explosion will happen to you in a year as long as you practice Part 1-Swim Across for 3-5 hours every day saving your sex energy".

In my first manuscript of Part 2-Astronaut, I had not written it to respect his private life. But, I think saving your sex energy as much as possible is the indispensable step for you to be able to become a psychic astronaut or accomplish something special. So, I dare add it.

★ The secret of big men's is having strong living vortexes which rotate and work on

Besides the vortex of your abdomen, other strong living vortexes of your physical body can shoot out immaterial strong fibers [the second attention, dream body] or the third attention. Strong living vortexes of your abdomen and of other parts of your physical body can send orders, messages, sounds, colors, smells, emotion, attack, or healing power to other people, animals, plants, trees, the unknown, another world, or the universe with these carried on the immaterial fiber, on the second attention or on the third attention.

That is to say, big men or those who have accomplished something, lived longer, grown more than 10-20 years younger, been happy, healthy, or been liked by many of the opposite sex, have good strong living vortexes which rotate and work on. The patriarch of Chinese Taoism says "One is wise who recognizes oneself as a stupid". But sometimes, I feel so regretful that I recognize I had lived in so-called hell for most of my life because my vortexes have barely begun to rotate automatically since the age of 50. Strangely, even the vortex on the surface of my chin sometimes rotates automatically now.

12. How cancer will happen after 3-5 year lump, stiff shoulder, and peculiar feeling in your fingers

★ Other dirty energy bodies, devils, and the floating immaterial above your head are giving you dirtiness, stickiness, fever, coldness, solidity, or numbness which can weaken you so as to kill you

If dirty energy bodies and devils often visit your vortex on the surface of your body or the inside of your body or stick to your body for a long time, your vortex will begin to rotate under groan the same as the fan rotates within sewage, sink, or mud. Furthermore, your aura around you, the energy channel of your internal organ, and your internal organ will become like sewage, sink or mud. As a result, more dirty energy bodies of others' and more devils will visit or stick to your vortex, energy channel, or internal organ, such as vultures, hyenas, or maggots.

The dirty, sticky, feverish, cold or solid immaterial [which is almost the world of the animal killed by you mercilessly and unnecessarily] begins to be floating above your head and your house, or around you, too. It is always connected with you through strong sticky wet immaterial pipe. Through this pipe, it can always run the dirty, sticky, feverish, cold or solid immaterial into you which can weaken or torture you. If you want to cure your or other's disease, or want to venture out to the universe, you have to be able to see this strong sticky wet immaterial pipe such as a strong floating anchor, cut it, and set yourself or others free.

Because of more attacks by dirty energy bodies, devils and the floating dirty, sticky, feverish, cold or solid immaterial, your vortex becomes like a fan in cold heavy oil, sludge, coal tar, cold clay, or solid snot. Then, your vortex can not rotate at all. Next, your energy channel which is connected with your dead useless vortex becomes cold and solid so that your energy channel is taken over by dirty energy bodies of others' and devils'. Your energy channel gets stuck by such as cold heavy oil, sludge, coal tar, cold clay, or solid snot. Such an energy channel looks like a snake which torture you or looks like a timber which Christ said about 2000 years ago. Tens of such energy channels like a snake hang down from your face, head, eyes and neck. Your vortex, your energy channel can neither run fresh, useful energy of the universe and of the earth and of the spirit into your internal organ, nor evacuate bad energy and devils from your internal organ.

At last, your internal organ which is connected with your dead, useless vortex and energy channel, becomes cold and solid. Your internal organ gets stuck by such as cold heavy oil, sludge, coal tar, cold clay, or solid snot, and becomes almost dead or useless.

★ Omens of death

If your heart is stuck, your face will become dirty black red and horizontal line [about half an inch] will appear between your eyes. Red spots may happen to the back of your neck, too. If your liver is stuck, upper nose will become dirty blue or black blue. If your lung is stuck, your face will become dirty white. If your spleen is stuck, your face will become dirty yellow. If your kidney is stuck, your face will become dirty black and you will feel lazy about your legs. In all cases, your face will lose beautiful gloss.

Lump happens to your internal organ. There may exist disordered part of spine just at the back of your weak internal organ. Violent sports [soccer, rugby, and so on], intense exercise, Yoga, long meditation, or accident is apt to injure your spine. Stiff shoulder, not-rotating neck, and the peculiar feeling of your fingers [a little pain, numb, impotent and so on] happen to you. Bad appetite, bad sleeping, bad bowel movement, and bad sex happen, too. Furthermore, your throat is apt to become weak or sore if you have divorced, been on bad terms with your wife or husband, or been much disappointed in love. It is because your throat is intimately connected with your sexual organ.

You are fearful of these warnings of your body. You go to 3-5 hospitals to check your body. But, nothing is problem with you in medical respect for 3-5 years. After that, cancer will happen to you, for example. As for heart disease or paralysis, it may happen to you in 1-6 months after these warnings of your body. A change for worse within your energy body, vortex, energy channel of your physical body and internal organ is, sticky->not glossy->fever->solid->cold->pass away. A change for better needs much wisdom and patience at least in 10 years. It is a big challenge. Trying a big challenge at your peril will surely make you much stronger, much wiser, patienter and modester little by little than before. Maybe, one of many challenges at your peril is how to emerge from unfortunate vicious circle and beckon the spirit that is written in Part 1-Swim Across.

If what I have written reminds you, you will owe me much gratitude as a lifesaver when you can emerge from unfortunate vicious circle. In such a case, I feel pleased that you will save other people instead of returning a favor to me.

The moment you succeed in cleaning up your dirty vortex and energy channel, the energy of your weak internal organ will begin to rotate violently suddenly horizontally or vertically and your weak internal organ begin to get well rapidly. You may hear a noise of crack within your head before the energy of your weak internal organ will begin to rotate for the first time.

13. How it took me 5-6 hours every night for 2 years to puff out the fever of depression about my old bitter love trouble

It is easy to erase your sticky immaterial like a soft jelly in your muscle, but it is very difficult to erase your sticky immaterial within your bones like a strong tenacious snake. I have been fighting against this strong tenacious snake since one and half an years ago.

It is very difficult to erase the fever of depression, too. It took me 5-6 hours every night from 1995 to 1997 to erase 80-90% of my fever of depression. Every night, I concentrated silently on my fever of depression whose color was black red brown, I puffed it out patiently together with my exhalation. My depressed emotion about my bitter love trouble of 33 years ago had lived in my fever of depression persistently. I had remembered my bitter love trouble naturally for 1-2 hours during 33 years.

I often felt so painful that I wanted to give up puffing out the fever of depression about my bitter love trouble. Whenever I was puffing out the fever of depression, I felt as if I soaked myself in a bathtub of warm urine. I carried through puffing out my fever of depression for 5-6 hours every night during 2 years patiently by all means. Now, I seldom remember my bitter love trouble.

★ In the universe, there is not the fever of depression such as steam of warm urine

Furthermore, I have become very sensitive to the fever of depression which belongs to other people, domestic animals, dog, garden tree, potted plants, or the crops. Almost whenever the energy body of other's touches me, I feel as if I were touched by a mop soaked in warm urine. At that time, I think I like more the bloodthirstiness of don Juan Matus' than other's fever of depression. There was not the fever of depression in don Juan Matus' bloodthirstiness when don Juan Matus got angry like a strong tiger. He understands me and smiles.

The picture which is drawn by Mr. Yamagata, a Japanese painter is very popular in U.S.A. I think his picture is colorful and beautiful, but I feel some fever of depression and some stickiness have remained in his picture. I think the feeling of his picture is that of inner space of the earth. The feeling of color in the far distant universe is cooler, drier, and glossier. Far distant universe has neither stickiness nor the fever of depression.

14. Why the etiquette of the energy body should be to touch others sparingly, although there are no manners, law, or police in the psychic world

You think there should be the same etiquettes in energy body world as those in the ordinary life after you have read my previously mentioned sentence. That is right.

The etiquettes about the energy body of human beings' are [1] don't enter into other body except for the purpose of healing of other body [2] don't stick to other thin immaterial film about a foot separate from other physical body for a long time [3] don't stick to the vortex of other physical body's, energy channel of other physical body, or other internal organ for a long time [4] don't blanket other physical body [5] don't hood other head or face [6] don't often visit other [7] respect other private life [8] don't peep at other sex scene or bathroom [9]do not peep at other toilet.

★ Gentlemen often behave like sly snakes, armed robbers, or thieves in the psychic world

Don Juan Matus says "A warrior touches the world around him sparingly. He doesn't take advantage of other people or animals or plants thoroughly not to receive the hostility from his surroundings".

Those, who are very polite, courteous, and decent in ordinary life, often don't follow the etiquettes about energy body at all. They are apt to break the etiquette although I teach the etiquettes many times. They are so proud that they think they can do anything without being noticed to do so. They are often like sly snakes, armed robbers or thieves.

★ Those who use herb are apt to stick to others or become crazy peepers

Those who use herb are apt to break the etiquettes about energy body. When they use herb, they can go out of their physical bodies and move to other people easily although they have dirty sticky energy body [dirty sticky energy bodies can neither go out of their physical bodies nor move to other people without using herb]. Their energy bodies are so sticky that they can not return to their physical bodies easily. Once their energy bodies stick to other people, they can not leave from other people easily and stay at other people for a long time because of their stickiness. Their energy bodies are often like a dirty strong paste. While their dirty energy bodies are sticking to other people, the physical bodies from which dirty energy bodies have gone out face the peril to be involved in traffic accident and so on.

Those who use herb are apt to be much interested in peeping at other private life, too. They are like crazy peepers. Crazy peepers have not the ability to see many devils who live in physical bodies of other people's. So, they like to stick to other physical bodies or like to enter into them secretively, too. 5 years ago I have begun to see many devils which live in me or in other. I have seen hundreds of black brown immaterial parasites in the intestine, immaterial snakes and so on in me, in other women or in other men. Beautiful young women often have many grim devils within her physical bodies. This experience has made me become modest and fairly detached from beautiful young women.

★ It needs much wisdom, patience and 2-3 secret weapons to deal with such rude energy bodies

Once you break such etiquettes in ordinary life, you will be renounced immediately or knocked down or receive exchange blows. If you break them about the man or woman a few times in succession, you will be arrested by the police. But, there is neither a law nor police in the psychic world. You have to have much wisdom, patience, and 2-3 secret weapons to deal with such rude energy bodies of others' if you want to survive in the psychic world.

★ Don't use such a merciless interlock for an extended period of time

If you are eager to touch other people, you had better touch softly for a while, at most 30 minutes-an hour. Don't use the likes of a pitchfork, strong fishhook, or claw of hawk's to touch other people. If you use such a merciless interlock for a long time, or even short time, other people will feel very painful or irritated. Such a manner is compared to sucking mother's milk and chewing on the nibble of the mother's breast.

★ Don't keep on knocking the door strongly-don't steal into broken wall

When you touch other people softly a few times and other people do not respond, you had better return to your physical body as soon as possible. Don't keep on using a merciless interlock against others for 3-6 hours or until the other responds to you or opens the gate to you. Such a manner can be compared to keeping on knocking at the door of someone's house's gate strongly for 3-6 hours or until the other opens the gate to you. If you do so, the other will call the police and you will be arrested. Or, don't try to steal through a broken wall of someone else or break through the gate of another energy body or of physical body. Such a manner can be compared to a sly snake, an armed robber or a thief.

★ I often prefer a devil to a human being because the devil is franker

In this respect, I am apt to like more a devil than the energy body of other human being's because the devil is not so persistent or rude as the energy body of other human being's. So, I do not beat the devil who is weaker than me thoroughly or mercilessly. Devil has some peculiar grace. For me, devil sometimes looks like a friend of naughty boys.

The devil is a master at disguise. He can approach us disguising itself as a lover, one-side lover, angel, the spirit, God, parent, child, beautiful woman, Christ or Buddha whom we believe in easily. Devil may be wiser than most of human beings. Sometimes, I had been tricked by the beautiful woman who was the devil disguised. Beautiful woman had often been snake devil. After I became suspicious and asked "Who are you?", the devil has never reappeared as a disguised beautiful woman. I think that the devil is franker than human beings.

15. The dreaming attention-the second attention which is like a sewage or diarrhea can move to other people

Whenever you visit someone else's house, you wash your face and wear your best or neat clothes. But in the psychic world, most of us often visit other people wearing dirty foul-smelling clothes with excrement, louse or infectious disease in company with devils. If your energy body is dirty, sticky, or feverish such as sewage, diarrhea or dirty paste, you had better stop to visit other people. You had better visit other people only when your energy body is beautiful, dry, not-sticky, cool, glossy, sweet, active as possible if you love other people at least.

The second attention [dreaming attention, energy body made of the second attention] is not so noble as the third attention. The second attention which is like a mud, sludge, heavy oil, can neither go out of the physical body nor move to other people easily [The first attention is like coal tar, cold clay, or solid snot]. But, when this second attention is warmed and purified by the light of the abdomen's or by concentrating on the breath so that it becomes more fluid like sewage, diarrhea or dirty paste, this second attention can go out of the physical body and move to other people. If the second attention that is like mud, sludge, or heavy oil was warmed by eating, drinking, or smoking herb, this second attention can go out of the physical body and move to other people, too. So to speak, a new devil is born.

Like don Juan Matus, the teacher of Mr, Carlos Castaneda, I think herb is useful for the clue for you to be able to go out of your physical body and move to other places for the first time. Furthermore, I think herb is useful for the last adjustments before you venture out to the universe. But, I think you had better not depend upon only herb. You had better strengthen and purify your energy body and physical body by other ways everyday, too.

★ Blanketing or hooding other physical body prevents other from absorbing noble energy from the universe or the spirit

Don't blanket other physical body with your energy body for long time. Don't hood other head or face with your energy body. If you do so, it is difficult for other to absorb noble energy from the universe or from the spirit. Furthermore, it is difficult for other to communicate with some area of the universe and the spirit.

16. Why these etiquettes should be applied to the world around you at least if you love it

I think the etiquettes about human energy body should be applied to animals, trees, plants, wind, fog, clouds, sea, rivers, insects, the earth, the moon, the sun, other stars and so on, as much as possible. I think they will become your friends if you can treat them as your friends.

★ Trees in a primeval forest is a teacher or benefactor for you

For example, I was much surprised to hear the voice of a tree for the first time. The soul of a tree is like a long rectangle within tree. I danced with hundreds of tree souls about 3 years ago. A tree is connected with other tree through beautiful yellow immaterial fiber each other. The tree in a primeval forest has more beautiful, sweeter, less sticky, less feverish energy than that of human being's or animal's. You have to study and absorb such tree's energy before you can enter into the universe. In this respect, a tree in a primeval forest is a teacher or a benefactor for you.

★ Seeing and sniffing the aura of stones can unveil the universe

At first, you should be able to see the aura of human being's. Next, you should be able to see the aura of tree's and plant's. Furthermore, You should be able to see the aura of stones, the sea, river, mountains, the earth, and other stars. If you can begin to see and sniff the aura of stone's, the hidden universe and infinity will begin to unveil before your eyes.

17.How a noble call-sign can beckon the ship of Egyptian Pyramid Text from the universe

Don Juan Matus, the teacher of Mr. Carlos Castaneda says in the book, The Power of Silence "Shamanism is journey of return. A warrior returns victorious to the spirit [the universe, knowledge, bird of freedom] having descended into hell. And from hell he brings trophies. Understanding is one of his trophies".

I think we can be compared to the birds which fall into a heavy oil sea or the space crafts which fall into swamp of sludge.

For 99% of time, I am confined in a heavy sea of oil or swamp of sludge, and I struggle to survive. I was not able to get rid of dirtiness, stickiness, fever, foul smelling, coldness, solidity or numbness completely. Some part of them has still remained in me. Or, could it be that I'm continuously, bitten by something or somebody like a vulture, hyena, or maggot.

For only 1 % of time, I am set free from the heavy sea of oil or swamp of sludge, and venture out of it. My call-sign [or my key word] sent to the far distant universe from the heavy sea of oil or swamp of sludge is something beautiful, not-sticky, cool, good smell, glossy, active, fluid, sweet, nimble, of abandon, of largess, and of humor as possible. I make my immaterial fiber or third attention carry such a call-sign to the far distant universe from my body. When I can succeed in communicating with the place in the far distant universe which has the same thing as that of my noble call sign, I can vomit heavy oil or sludge, and shut out heavy oil or sludge. At that time, something more beautiful, not-sticky, cool, good smell, glossy, active, fluid, sweet, nimble, of abandon, of largess, and of humor, begins to flow down to me abundantly from the far distant universe. Immaterial cylinder about 7 feet in diameter descends to me from the sky at times.

★ The ship is something that flows down to me abundantly from the universe

I use something flowing down abundantly from the far distant universe as the wing of bird or the special fuel of a spacecraft. I think something descending abundantly from the far distant universe or immaterial cylinder from the sky is the ship which is described in the Ancient Egyptian Pyramid Text. I think the Egyptian king or ancient psychic astronauts embarked on it before the death of their physical body and departed to the universe.

Furthermore, I think this ship is the spirit. The spirit will descend to you as a shower, dark gold dust, fog, bullet, tornado, cannon-shell, balloon, babble, big fire, sea, cylinder, solid mass, emptiness and so on if you can send the feeling of abandon, largess, humor to the spirit and the universe. If you see, speak and act in such a way, the spirit will notice you, welcome you, touch you and give an accurate information to you.

# Part 3

## Stare Effect

Stare can bring up the beautiful strong red energy of heart so that you can lose undependable self-image and self-pity. The beautiful strong red energy of heart can burn or shut out dirty energies of other people and of devils which have stolen into your body. As a result, you can shoot out your useful immaterial fiber or the third attention to an object and realize what you imagine. Don Juan Matus says "Without it, we are sediment or nothing". Then, Silent voice (voice without voice) and overwhelming premonition will happen to you little by little and you will have dependable self-importance and trust in yourself.

1. Stare at leaves' interspace, stone or star everyday for an hour for 10 years with the space between your eyebrows broadened

2. Everyday stare can make you see or shoot out your immaterial fiber or your third attention to an object. Your third attention is a phenix or the inner spirit.

3. The third attention is like a smoke in treasure-chest. People who have neither it nor immaterial fibers can be compared to a toothless tiger in Africa

4. One who can stop one's breath automatically can attain anything

5. Can stop your internal dialogue just before shooting out your immaterial fiber or your third attention

6. Can see and catch on the spirit after you can see stone's aura

7. The beautiful black spirit can give you patience, originality, and bravery

8. Only from healthy strong internal organ, your immaterial fiber can be shot out

9. Go into stupidity-inefficiency and return to wisdom-efficiency intentionally many times to be able to distinguish one from another

10. To make your immaterial fiber or your third attention not weaken, you had better shoot out it at least once everyday or catch on much stronger spirit as possible. Medicine for you

11. I was nearly killed by the strong spirit and exploded to pieces

12. Return the favor to a tree

NEXT Text

1. Stare at leaves' interspace, stone or star everyday for an hour for 10 years with the space between your eyebrows broadened

Shamanism, the spirit, the strong immaterial fiber from body, the third attention, Carlos Castaneda's books, Ancient Egyptian Pyramid Text, Cabala, The Emerald-Tablet of Thoth, Yoga Sutra can understand not by reading but by experience.

If you want to understand them, you had better stare at something for 30 minutes-an hour everyday for 10 years, practicing Part 1-Swim Across (involving Tensegrity) or strengthening your energy body by Chinese military arts as possible. By it, you will be able to begin to twinkle a beautiful immaterial fire (light ) in your body and keep on staring patiently everyday for 10 years.

As the book, The Second Ring of Power by Mr.Carlos Castaneda in 1977 says, you had better stare at the interspace between the leaves of a tree in a primeval forest or of a tree which has not been planted by human being->stare at the stone or rock which you like->stare at the star which you like.

Whenever you can not realize what you imagine or think of, your body has been taken over by dirty energy bodies of other people or devils. As a result, the red energy of your heart has weakened and the fire within your abdomen has gone out. You feel stuck, irritated, depressed or gloomy. Then, bad complexion, bad bowel movement and stiff shoulder have happened to you. In such case, you can not shoot out your immaterial fiber or third attention to an outside object nor judge-control it. That is to say, you have undependable self-importance or indulge in self-pity. The origin of joy and of self-confidence is a strong beautiful red energy of your heart. You have lost joy and self-confidence because the red energy of your heart has weakened.

Strong beautiful red energy of heart can be compared to a burning stove. Dirty energy bodies and devils can be compared to a fly. If a stove is burning, a fly can not stick to a stove.

Strong beautiful red energy of heart can burn or shut out dirty energy bodies and devils which have stolen into or stuck to your body. Stare at something with your eyebrows broadened can bring up the strong beautiful red energy of your heart so that you can have joy, self-confidence, and good complexion. As a result, the strong beautiful red energy of your heart can burn or shut out dirty energy bodies of other people and devils. Dirty energy bodies of other people and devils can not make your immaterial fiber or third attention confined to your body.

Then, You can shoot out your immaterial fiber or third attention to an outside object so that you can realize what you imagine or think of. That is to say, You can lose undependable self-importance, undependable self-image, undependable trust and self-pity. You can have dependable self-importance, dependable self-image and dependable trust.

The strong beautiful red energy of your heart looks like a strong fortress or castle for you, too. Silent voice (voice without voice) and overwhelming premonition will happen to you little by little. Following them, you will become healthier-happier-more efficient and more grateful. You will never die of cancer. Besides stare at something, strengthening your small intestine, bladder and lung can bring up the strong beautiful red energy of your heart. To strengthen your small intestine, you have to make your bowel movement better.

2. Everyday stare can make you see or shoot out your immaterial fiber or your third attention to an object. Your third attention is a phenix or the inner spirit

By and by, you can understand something that shoots out from the vortex on the surface of your body, and can catch on the object you stare at. Something is immaterial fiber which shoots out from your body. Mr.Carlos Castaneda's teacher, don Juan Matussays "We are sediment or nothing without strong immaterial fibers".

Furthermore, you will be able to see the aura of human being's, of animal's, and of tree's. At last, you will be able to see the aura of stone's, of rock's, of mountain's, river's, of sea's, of the ground's and of star's without using herbs.

After such a phenomenon, you may be able to feel that something beautiful, dry, glossy, sweet, kind, cool, active, nimble, fierce, peaceful, fluid and noble, will flow out of your body abundantly to the object which you stare at or think about.

Such something is the third attention that can be compared to the inner spirit of yours or Phenix called God in Egypt. The third attention is much subtler, fainter than immaterial fiber which shoots out of your body. But, it is much stronger and nimbler than immaterial fiber. It has stronger attack-power and healing-power than immaterial fiber. It can penetrate into or break through anything or any place immediately. It can travel to 2 billion light year distant-universe almost within a second. It is the origin of a seer, too. The origin of blue third attention is your healthy liver, the origin of red third attention is your healthy heart, the origin of yellow third attention is your healthy spleen, the origin of white third attention is your healthy lung, the origin of transparent third attention is your healthy V-spot on the crest of the sternum at the base of your neck, the origin of black third attention is your healthy kidney.

3.The third attention is like a smoke in treasure-chest. People who have neither it nor immaterial fibers can be compared to a toothless tiger in Africa

It is very difficult for us to confirm the existence of our subtle faint third attentions. The third attention can be compared to the smoke in a treasure-chest. Happy, healthy, or successful people have active useful third attention and use it in everyday life unconsciously. But, maybe, they will be at a loss about how to emerge from misfortune if they fall into misfortune and make their third attention dead and useless. They do not know how to make their third attention revive and work on for them again. Unhappy, unhealthy, or unfortunate people have dead useless third attention and have not made it work on for them unconsciously, so that they can not recognize the existence of the third attention at all. People who have not active useful third attention or immaterial fiber can be compared to a toothless tiger in Africa or a soldier without a gun on a battlefield.

4. One who can stop one's breath automatically can attain anything

Your active useful third attention can go out of your body and work on for you only while your breath is stopping automatically. Your breath is apt to stop automatically when you feel so happy that you want nothing and do not want to accomplish anything. If you want to confirm the existence of the third attention, you had better rent a house at your best power-spot place and keep on concentrating on your breath at your peril everyday there for 3 weeks. You will experience hotness, coldness, shiver, pain, big explosion and big automatic whirl in your body. After 2 weeks you will be able to feel happy and stop your breath automatically. Then, your active useful third attention will begin to go out of your body and work on for you.

Indian Yoga book says "One who can stop one's breath automatically can attain or accomplish anything. You had better practice stopping your breath automatically several times everyday". How to stop breath automatically has been written in Part 1-Swim Across. If you are an American, you can challenge it at your peril when you are fired or change your job. I think you can clean up your life and appreciate my kindness. I have challenged it 5 times.

5. Can stop your internal dialogue just before shooting out your immaterial fiber or your third attention

Just before you can shoot out your immaterial fiber or the third attention from your body to the object which you stare at, concentrate on or think about, you have to stop your internal dialogue and enter into the peculiar inner silence or the peculiar happiness for a while. The feeling of stopping internal dialogue is such as putting a car into neutral or your being suspended .If you keep on staring at something everyday with the space between your eyebrows broadened, you will be able to stop your internal dialogue sooner or later and be able to shoot out your immaterial fiber or third attention to an outside object.

Stopping your internal dialogue, peculiar inner silence and peculiar happiness happen to you whenever you can stop your breath automatically. Then, you can shoot out your immaterial fiber or third attention to an object and judge-control it so that you can attain anything. Personal power is a lucky feeling or mood which can be brought about by stopping your internal dialogue and by stopping your breath automatically. You can stop your internal dialogue and your breath automatically easily when good complexion, good appetite, good sleeping, good bowel movement, good sex, soft shoulder, rejuvenation, moderate eating, good waist and subtle breath happen to you.

6. Can see and catch on the spirit after you can see stone's aura

After you can begin to see the aura of stone, you will be able to see something that is floating in the inner space, within the earth, or in the universe. Something is the spirit. It is blue, red, yellow, white, transparent, green, black, or orange. It is beautiful, dry, glossy, sweet, kind, cool, active, nimble, peaceful, fluid, noble, fierce, of abandon, of largess, and of humor.

At the beginning, your immaterial fiber [your second attention] may catch on many devils because your immaterial fiber is still dirty. Your immaterial fiber does not deserve to catch on the spirit. Furthermore, you may be tricked by devils and catch on many disguised devils because you are quite a stranger to another world.

If you keep on staring at something and practicing Part 1-Swim Across (involving Tensegrity), or strengthening your energy by Chinese military arts everyday patiently so that you can become much healthier, feel much happier than before, your immaterial fiber will become beautiful, dry, glossy, sweet, kind, cool, active, nimble, peaceful, fluid, noble, fierce and of abandon, of largess, and of humor. Then, your immaterial fiber will begin to catch on the spirit. Or, your third attention will begin to catch on the spirit.

7. The beautiful black spirit can give you patience, originality, and bravery

The black spirit is often mistaken for devil. Dirty black one is one of devils. But, beautiful glossy one is the spirit which can give patience, originality and bravery to human being. It makes your bones strong, too. You will become arrogant if you absorb much energy of black spirit's through your kidney. You will be a rotten female or rotten apple if you can absorb little energy of black spirit's. The yellow spirit can give you sweet. It makes your muscles healthy, beautiful, and strong. The yellow spirit is said to be the most important among the spirits. Such saying is not correct. If you stick to the yellow spirit and keep on absorbing only its energy too much, your abdomen will expand. You will feel irritated and often break wind. However nutritious and delicious food is, you will become bore, irritated, depressed, or unhealthy if you keep on eating it everyday for long time. That is the same. I hate the yellow spirit still now because I absorbed the energy of yellow spirit's too much a year ago.

The red spirit has ruthless and joyful energy, the blue spirit has cunning energy, the black spirit has patient and brave energy, and the yellow spirit has sweet energy.

8. Only from healthy strong internal organ, your immaterial fiber can be shot out

You can shoot out strong red immaterial fiber or the third attention from healthy heart, catch on the red spirit, and absorb ruthless joyful energy from the red spirit. You can shoot out strong blue immaterial fiber or the third attention from your healthy liver, catch on the blue spirit and absorb cunning energy from the blue spirit. You can shoot out strong black immaterial fiber or the third attention from your healthy kidney, catch on the black spirit, and absorb patient energy from the black spirit. You can shoot out strong yellow immaterial fiber or the third attention from your healthy spleen, catch on the yellow spirit, and absorb sweet energy from the yellow spirit.

When your immaterial fiber or your third attention succeeds in contacting the spirit, the spirit will run something beautiful, dry, glossy, sweet, kind, cool, active, nimble, fluid, noble, fierce, of abandon, of largess, and of humor into you abundantly to strengthen, purify, heal or cure you. Such something is colorful or transparent. Then, the spirit begins to give you the ability to become a psychic astronaut, too.

9. Go into stupidity-inefficiency and return to wisdom-efficiency intentionally many times to be able to distinguish one from another

You have to be aware whether you are stupid or wise. You have to be able to distinguish your inefficiency from your efficiency. When you are taken over by dirty energy bodies of others' and by devils and you get stuck, you can not shoot out the immaterial fiber or the third attention from your body so that you are stupid and inefficient. You look like a timid, stingy, gloomy man or woman. Then, you feel unhappy, sad, depressed, irritated, lonely, lazy, and impotent. You can not realize what you imagine. You ignore your body-response or do not wait your body-response. A beautiful immaterial light does not twinkle in your body so that your energy body is dirty, sticky, feverish, cold or solid. Bad complexion, bad appetite, bad bowel movement, poor or flabby abdomen, eating too much, bad sleeping, bad sex, stiff shoulder and rough breath have happened to you.

When you are taken over neither by dirty energy bodies of others' nor by devils and do not get stuck, you can shoot out the immaterial fiber or the third attention from your body so that you are wise and efficient. You look like a man or woman of abandon, of largess, and of humor. Then, you feel happy, peaceful, silent, active and powerful. You can accomplish something naturally following your body-response (which is written in Part 5-Body-Response). A beautiful immaterial light twinkles in your body so that your energy body is beautiful, dry, cool, or fluid. Good complexion, good appetite, good bowel movement, moderate eating, soft and firm abdomen, good sleeping, good sex, flexibility of your body, and subtle breath have happened to you.

To be able to distinguish inefficiency from efficiency, you had better go into stupidity and inefficiency, and return to wisdom and efficiency intentionally many times. You had better be taken over by dirty energy bodies of others', by devils, or by women's energy bodies, and shut out them intentionally many times. You had better catch on devil or the spirit by turns intentionally many times. Furthermore, you had better remember your failures and successes in your life in detail as possible at least 100 times, too.

Hey ! According to the above-mentioned sentence, you had better test now whether or not your plan or idea (about money, work, post, opposite sex, friend, parents, son, daughter or health) can be realized sooner or later. In most cases, you can become aware that you have been confined to an undependable false plan or idea which is one of so-called hells on the earth.

Needless to say, I have been confined to many such hells for long years. I have gone into stupidity-inefficiency and returned to wisdom-efficiency unconsciously many times. I have remembered my failures and successes in detail in my life as many as possible, so I can barely have distinguished stupidity-inefficiency from wisdom-efficiency. As a result, I can have written about how to distinguish one from another to you. I feel I have paid many tuition fees for long years because of my stupidity and stubbornness.

10. To make your immaterial fiber or your third attention not weaken, you had better shoot out it at least once everyday or catch on much stronger spirit as possible. Medicine for you

After such a study, you have to be able to shoot out your strong immaterial fiber or the third attention from your body by all means when you have to be alert, wise, and efficient. Happy, healthy or successful people can do so. You had better shoot out it from your body at least once everyday. If you do not do so everyday, it will apt to become weak and almost dead, useless.

Gradually you will be aware that you can easily shoot out your strong immaterial fiber or the third attention to the object to which you have body-response such as (1) you begin to feel relieved and relaxed (2) begin to take a deep breath (3) stiff abdomen turns to be fluid and relaxed.

Consulting our own interests, most of us decide what to do or whether or not we make friends with someone or whether or not we marry someone without following our comfortable body-response. Most of us just have to do anything. Most of us are not content to do. In such a case, our immaterial fibers or third attention are apt to be confined to our body so that we fail in realizing what we imagine or think of or plan. If we do so in succession, our immaterial fibers or third attention become almost dead and useless. Our immaterial fibers' or the third attention's being confined to our bodies for long time can weaken our bodies and hearts.

Then, most of us begin to have bad complexion, bad bowel movement, bad appetite, bad sleeping, bad sex and stiff shoulder. Happy lucky feeling (light spring breeze, cunning, ruthless, abandon, largesse, humor, joy, smooth, clarity, peace, sweetness, kindness, patience, detachment, rushing headlong) runs away from our eyes, voice and behaviors so that we can not beckon the spirit, too. We become a toothless tiger. Most of us look like a slavery of money, food, post, fame or sex. In this respect, I have often failed because I have followed not my comfortable body-response but only my own interests. So, you had better not make a decision only according to your own interests such as money, post, living, fame and sex. Following your comfortable body-response, you had better do as possible what you are content to do.

Now, you can understand "Shooting out your immaterial fiber or third attention from your body is medicine for you. It can give you joy, pleasure and mercy, too. It is (1) the Buddhist precepts (2) or the path of enlightenment (3) or supernatural power (4) or stopping your breath automatically (5) or comfortable body-response (6) or vanishing your pains and bad feeling (7) or shutting out dirty shadow (8) or vanishing devils and dirty energy of yours and of others (9) or fusing with something (10) or silent knowledge (11) or realizing what you imagine easily (16) or dependable trust", can't you?

It is the sentence of the book which was written in Chinese 2000 years ago by the prince of the big country just above Iran. He went to China and translated the teaching of Buddha into Chinese, explained it and wrote the book in China. It was very difficult for me to understand his book at the beginning 10 years ago. But, comfortable body-response happened to me. The core of my abdomen turned to be very hot and I felt as if all my body were burning while reading his book. I had been staring at his book everyday since then as if I were solving a complicated puzzle. It took me 3 years to translate his book into Japanese, explain it and write the book with the title-How to concentrate on your breath and stop it automatically (in Japanese) 7 years ago.

I think most readers feel comfortable body-response such as feeling relieved or relaxed while reading my book even though most reader seldom understand my book at the beginning. But, gradually most readers will be able to enjoy trying to understand my book further with the help of their immaterial fibers or third attention (body-response) as if most readers were solving a complicated puzzle. You can practice shooting your immaterial fiber or third attention and can bring up dependable trust while staring at and reading my book as many times as possible. Whenever you stare at my book, can shoot out your immaterial fiber or third attention to my book from your body and can understand some sentence of my book correctly and deeply, some comfortable body-response happens to you. Then, your assemblage point(the core of your consciousness) breaks through the point of no self-pity and moves to the interior of undoubt in your body. You can trust in "I can surely understand some sentence of this book without a plausible reason." This is the way to read the letters of the ancient remains without dictionary, too. The future of your life looks like the letters of the ancient remains. So, you had better apply such a way to reading the future of your life.

Furthermore, you had better make friends with danger or death at your peril. When you run a risk at your peril, you can easily shoot out immaterial fiber or the third attention from your body. Happy, healthy or successful people prefer running a risk. They are apt to like dangerous hobbies, too. They look like gentlemen and naughty boys. Unhappy, unhealthy, unsuccessful people are like rotten apples and do not prefer running a risk at their perils. In most of cases, the origin of rotten apples may be the shortage of beautiful glossy black energy and weak kidney.

Immaterial fiber or the third attention is compared to a young beautiful woman or a snake that lives in your body by Indian Yoga book. Yoga book says "You had better move young woman or snake in your body everyday".

To strengthen your immaterial fiber or your third attention, you had better strengthen your physical body and energy body everyday and had better be able to catch on much stronger spirit as possible. The strength of the spirit is proportionate to the degree of the spirit's beauty, gloss, coolness, fluid, kindness, nimbleness, dignity, sweet, bloodthirstiness, nobleness, fierceness, abandon, largess, and humor.

11. I was nearly killed by the strong spirit and exploded to pieces

For much stronger spirit, you are a nuisance because you are still dirty, sticky, feverish, cold, numb, rude, coward, stingy, or gloomy. It takes devil 3-5 years to kill you. It takes the strong spirit less than a second to kill you if the strong spirit dislikes or hates you very much.

I was nearly killed by the strong spirit about a year ago. When I concentrated on some strong spirit within the earth, my energy body was suddenly exploded to pieces and enlarged more than the size of the earth within a second as a thin film. So, I coiled round the earth not to be flowed away to the universe, and then could compress my thin energy body. If I had been fainted, I might have been killed.

I had been so proud and careless that I thought there was no danger for me within the earth. I had become to make light of the inner earth. Then, I was nearly killed. Don Juan Matus, the teacher of Mr. Carlos Castaneda says "We have to save sex energy as possible to survive in another world. We will be exploded to pieces, can not compress our energy bodies, and be killed if we have not plentiful sex energy". I can have confirmed his saying is right. I have been saving sex energy as possible since a few years ago, so I could barely compress my energy body and barely survive.

I can see clearly that my immaterial fiber or my third attention can be shot out to the universe straightly from my body at super high-speed without bending or falling like a gun, a missile, an eagle or a hawk after I have saved my sex energy for more than a few month. A female ally, female angel or spirit notices my flying immaterial fiber or my third attention and often descends to me at super high-speed all the way from the far distant universe. In such a case, I often think in secret that I do not need women who have physical bodies any more, or I wonder why I had been lewd for long years or I wonder why I have married. My wife can not read English, so I can have written such a sentence in English in this book.

12. Return the favor to a tree

we have to understand that we are giving a nuisance to a tree while we are staring at the interspace between a tree's leaves for 30 minutes-an hour. The tree feels painful, irritated or depressed because we are still dirty, sticky, feverish, cold, solid, numb, or rude. We can absorb less dirty, less sticky, less feverish, less cold, less solid, less numb, or less rude energy from a tree. A tree is a benefactor for us. So, we had better return the favor to a tree. At least, we had better not cut or break a tree mercilessly and unnecessarily from now on. If we can treat a tree as our friend as possible, it will turn to be our friend.

For the spirit or a tree, we are like a devil. We had better become modester. For the earth, we are not more important or nobler than a tree. We only take and take from the earth, and soil the earth. We have not returned the favor to the earth.

While you are staring at an object, you had better touch or penetrate into softly for a short time. You had better absorb the precious energy of object's a little. Don't use and squeeze it until it has shriveled to nothing.

# Part 4

---

## Erase Stickiness

Your third attention is like a smoke in a treasure-chest. How to recognize and handle it for you.Erasing stickiness make it appear from your body.

1. Dry rustling energy body can break through sticky inner space to the universe and shut out devils

2. Complaint gives you stickiness and stickiness makes you unhealthy-unhappy-inefficient

3. Bad relationship with opposite sex? was the origin of Napoleon's downfall and of Carlos Castaneda's not becoming the successor to don Juan Matus?

4. As for me, the complaint about my parents and my old bitter trouble had let me fall into heavy Oil Sea for long years so that they had made my third attention almost dead

5. Sticky pus' pouch's explosion and my forehead's collapse have made my third attention barely revive since about 10 years ago

6.You can be conscious of the moment you shoot out your super high-speed third attention to a star

7. Extreme coldness and extreme hotness of the universe are the origins of the sacred and of power

8. To get used to the harsh universe and strengthen your third attention, you have to absorb dry inorganic energy from stones and stars

9. Cut floating sticky pipes to set yourself and other free

10. Subtle third attention can be compared to a smoke in a treasure-chest. How to handle it?

11. The feeling of opposite sex can teach you where to go

12. Successful people make their third attention work on for them unconsciously, but will be at a loss how to revive it

13. To strengthen himself, my young successor (?) will have to fall into heavy oil sea and venture out of it intentionally many times

14. Like a danger to erase stickiness

NEXT Text

1. Dry rustling energy body can break through sticky inner space to the universe and shut out devils

The earth is coiled round by something such as immaterial melted plastic. Inner space is like a band of immaterial melted plastic. Such something flows from the south to the north on the surface of the earth like a large river about at speed of a foot per second.

When sunbeam begins to hit the margin of the band just before sunrise, the band sings a song like thousands of birds. Sunbeam begins to invade into the band and makes the smell of something burning emit in the band. Some part of the sunbeam can not break though the band, and is divided on the margin of the band. It engulfs the margin of the band. The band of the earth is very sticky. The band of the earth seems to prevent the earth from bursting. This band is equal to the sticky first attention of human being's body.

If you want to venture out to the rustling and dry universe, you have to be able to break through such sticky inner space. If your energy body is sticky, it can not break through sticky inner space. Your sticky energy body is caught in the sticky inner space. Dirty energy bodies of others' and devils can give you stickiness. If your energy body is rustling and dry, it can break through sticky inner space. When you make your rustling dry energy body break through the rim of sticky inner space, you feel as if you broke through the thin layer of ice or of glass.

★ Stare at stones-stars and practice the ways of Yoga to erase stickiness

Tree, stone, star can give you rustle and dryness. So, you had better stare at tree, stone, or star with your eyebrows broadened everyday for 30 minutes-an hour for 10 years practicing some proper body exercises. For example, some proper body exercises have been written in Part 1-Swim Across, and in Yoga book. To erase your stickiness, Yoga book recommends(1) swallow down 3 m 50cm long cloth slowly and draw it under the supervision of the teacher (2) inject water into anus and move the muscle of abdomen (3) insert a piece of string into nose and draw it from mouth (4) stare at a small object until you shed tears (5) turn the muscle of abdomen (6) breathe fast like bellows.

If you practice the above mentioned content, you will be able to begin to shoot out your immaterial fiber or the third attention from your body, catch on tree, stone, or star through it, and absorb the rustling and dry energy from tree, stone, or star. Your immaterial fiber or your third attention will become less sticky and more rustling and drier.

After you can shoot out rustling and dry energy body from your physical body, you will be able to let it break through the sticky inner space and fly into the far distant rustling and dry universe immediately.

★ Devils like stickiness, but the spirits like rustle and dryness

Furthermore, you can shut out dirty energy bodies of others' and devils if you begin to have more rustling or dry energy. Dirty energy bodies of other' and devils can neither live in rustling and dry energy nor stick to rustling and dry energy. They hate rustling and dry energy and like sticky energy. So, they live in or stick to sticky energy bodies of men's or of women's, and sticky inner space.

The spirit hates sticky energy bodies of men's or of women's, and sticky inner space. It likes rustling and dry energy bodies of men's or of women's, rustling, dry universe and inner earth. A power-spot on the earth has a hole and is connected with the rustling, dry universe by the long energy cylinder. So, power-spot is not sticky. The spirit is floating at a power spot on the earth, too.

2. Complaint gives you stickiness and stickiness makes you unhealthy-unhappy-inefficient

Besides dirty energy bodies of others' and devils, complaint has given you stickiness. There are many kinds of complaints. I think the second or third biggest complaint is the bad relationship with opposite sex, or with son or daughter. Disease is the first biggest complaint. I think the bad relationship with parents is the fourth biggest complaint. The fifth biggest one is the complaint about work, money and post.

I think there exists fair impartiality about complaint. Most of us have a certain complaint more or less. We can have neither all good fortunes nor all misfortunes. Those who have been proud of their good fortunes are apt to ruin in 3-5 years, at the latest in 10 years.

I think the bad relationship with an opposite sex is the second biggest obstacle to become a psychic astronaut or to become healthy or efficient.

★ Divorce and disappointed love bring about cancer easily

If one has divorced or lost a big love, one will be given much stickiness by it. One will be given much stickiness by the bad relationship with a spouse and the death of a spouse, too. Stickiness will make one's vortexes on the surface of one's body, the energy channels of one's internal organ, internal organ and the central energy pipe of one's body get stuck.

So, beautiful immaterial light will go out and not be able to twinkle in one's body. Bad complexion, bad appetite, bad bowl movement, bad sleeping, bad sex, stiff shoulder will happen. Intimately throat is connected with sex organ through energy channel. So, one's throat is apt to become sore or a malign tumor because of the bad relationship with opposite sex. One's voice is apt to become bad. One will feel unhappy, lonely, depressed, irritated. One's immaterial fiber of one's body will become almost dead and useless. One can not shoot out one's immaterial fiber from one's body, so that one can not catch on the spirit which can give human being happiness-health-ability. Needless to say, one can not shoot out the third attention from one's body. Cancer is apt to happen, sooner or later.

3. Bad relationship? with opposite sex was the origin of Napoleon's downfall and of Carlos Castaneda's not becoming the successor to don Juan Matus?

I think Mr,Carlos Castaneda could not have become the successor to don Juan Matus, the teacher of Mr. Carlos Castaneda because he parted from the woman who had his child. Although he was taught how to get rid of his stickiness by don Juan Matus, he seemed to be unable to have gotten rid of his stickiness almost completely. Besides stickiness, the bad relationship with the opposite sex (?) seemed to have given him the fever of depression, coldness, and numbness, too.

I think the big origin of Napoleon's downfall was his divorce from his wife whom he loved. His wife could not have his baby, so he divorced although he loved her. She seemed to be a flirt, too. The sadness gave him considerable stickiness and the fever of depression. His abdomen got stuck by stickiness and fever, and become weak, so his abdomen often itched. The itch made his immaterial fiber or his third attention weak and undependable. With weak and undependable one, he nearly became like a toothless tiger. I imagined about him staring at his coffin in Paris.

★ Lack of sex energy makes our immaterial fibers bend and fall

If we are intimate with opposite sex, we can not save our sex energy. If we are not full of sex energy, we will lose the same noble fierceness as that of a young hawk so that we can not break through the sticky inner space. If we can shoot out the immaterial fiber or the third attention from our bodies, it will be apt not to go straight but to bend and fall. It can not reach an object. A moderate relationship with a spouse is apt to give subtle stickiness. It is very difficult for us to be conscious of subtle stickiness and to get rid of it. It can be compared to alloy in fuel.

★ Sad sticky womb

Although some American woman has been practicing Inca-style body exercise called Tensegrity earnestly for long years as to teach it to others, she had had much sad stickiness in her womb until 2 years ago. When I met her 2 years ago, I was much surprised to find that her womb was full of sad stickiness. As soon as I made her get rid of it, the strong noble white immaterial fiber shot out from her body to the sky. So, I led her white fiber to the white roof of the universe. Then, asking don Genaro to take care of her, I connected her white fiber with don Genaro. Don Genaro began to glitter suddenly.

4. As for me, the complaint about my parents and my old bitter trouble had let me fall into heavy Oil Sea for long years so that they had made my third attention almost dead

Like Napoleon, my father was beaten not by a gun or sword but by the bad relationship with opposite sexes. My father was a lieutenant of Japan army and very brave in a battlefield. But, after World War 2, he got stuck by much stickiness because of the bad relationship with my mother.

My father's first wife died in childbirth. My father loved his first wife very much. My mother is a second wife of my father. After World War 2, my father took it out on and often outraged our family. My father died in poverty 31 years ago when I was 28 years old. When he died, I did not feel sad at all. But, I can have understood and forgiven him little by little for 31 years.

As I have written in Part 2-Astronaut, it took me 5-6 hours every night for 2 years [1997-1998] to puff out the fever of depression and stickiness about my old bitter love trouble. Concentrating on my breath every night for 2 years, I puffed out them little by little in my house by 1998. I had rented other's house for a month and concentrated on my breath there everyday for 3 weeks. Although I had done so 5 times by 1997, I could gotten rid of neither the fever of my depression nor my stickiness about my old bitter trouble. Furthermore, I had been apt to take it out on my family [wife and 4 children] the same as my father did.

As for me, the complaints about my parents and my old bitter trouble had been the second or the third biggest origin of stickiness for long years. They had been depriving me of joy, peace, and ability for long years. They had made me unhealthy, stupid and inefficient for long years. They had let me fall into heavy Oil Sea or hell.

★ My third attention gave me instinct when I threw as a pitcher in boyhood, but almost died because of my complaint for long years

I could not have confirmed the existence of my third attention before I began to read Mr, Carlos Castaneda's books since 7 years ago. My female ally visited me twice shaking the ceiling of my hometown house when I was 10 or 11 year old boy. In those days when I played a baseball as a pitcher in the playground of the elementary school, I could know every ball's destination and direction 3 feet in front of every batter. Before a batter swung a bat, I could know where to go about every ball correctly which I threw. It lasted for two days. I was so frighten that I ran away to my house thinking why?

When I played a baseball as a pitcher, my third attention shot out from my body to a batter and made me know the destination and direction of every ball beforehand. Then, my third attention brought me silent knowledge. The subtler the third attention is, the more efficient it is. It can be compared to smoke in a treasure-chest. In most cases one who has active useful third attention can not be conscious of its shooting out from one's body. One thinks something special and mysterious has worked on for one. One may think such something is God or a good fortune. Before the third attention begins to shoot out and work on, stopping of the internal dialogue and peculiar inner silence have to happen even when one moves, works, plays, talks, hears, eats, sniffs, sings, goes to stool, and makes love. Because I threw a ball without internal dialogue, I could handle my third attention. In such a case, I emitted something from my body, sank into inner silence and fused with the energy of the surroundings.

As I became in my late teens, I became very sensitive to the bad relationship between my father and my mother. They often quarreled and talked about their divorce. My father often outraged my family involving me. I often thought I tried to disappear from my hometown house, but I stopped. I thought I had to be patient in my hometown house in Kyoto Prefecture in Japan until I graduated from high school.

I entered Osaka City University and left my hometown house in Kyoto Prefecture. My grandmother living with my parents committed a suicide by throwing herself to the river before I graduated from it. I barely graduated from it earning money for myself and began to live in Tokyo, Japan Capital City at the age of 22. Just after I began to live in Tokyo, I experienced the bitter trouble.

5. Sticky pus' pouch's explosion and my forehead's collapse have made my third attention barely revive since about 10 years ago

The complaints about my parents and my bitter love trouble had been giving me much stickiness and deprived me of joy, happy feeling, peace, inner silence so that I had made my third attention almost dead and useless. I had remembered the complaints about them for 2-4 hours everyday for about 30-34 years. I had been foolish enough to waste time on the destructive for 2-4 hours for long years. When I rented a house in mountains at the age of 45 about 14 years ago, I concentrated only on my breath everyday for 3 weeks. Then, something like a pouch of sticky bloody pus exploded suddenly in my body. A pouch of sticky bloody pus was full of my complaint about my parents. Since then, my complaint about my parents has almost disappeared.

At the age of 50 about 9 years ago, I rented a house at a fishing harbor and concentrated on my breath everyday for 3 weeks. Then, I felt the part just above the center of my eyebrows collapsed and a small hole appeared.

A small hole's diameter was about an inch. So, I could begin to feel spacious and less sticky. I felt as if I went out of a harbor to a vast ocean for the first time. I could begin to be engulfed by manlier atmosphere. This part of the forehead is called a sex organ or a white noble bird in Indian Yoga, too. I can feel my sex energy ascents to it and feel the smell of my sex energy from it. I think my third attention has barely begun to work on again since then after an interval of 40 years. Sometimes, the idea which glances off me is realized.

★ To be realized 10 times in succession makes me feel weird and fearful

The third attention is very strange and odd. When my third attention works on very well and the ideas which glanced off me have been realized 10-20 times in succession, I feel weird and fearful. When the ideas about society and big disasters which glanced off me have been realized 10-20 times in succession, I feel as if I become the almighty God. I feel more weird and fearful. I want to throw the almighty God away. I want to throw my third attention away. When my third attention does not work on at all, I fail 10-20 times in succession. Then, I feel missing my third attention. I hope my third attention will work on for me again.

When my third attention works on well, my energy body and my physical body are not sticky. I do not feel I get stuck. Then, I feel happy, healthy, satisfied, light, peaceful, silent. To be sure, good complexion, good appetite, good bowl movement and subtle breath have to have happened to me before my third attention works on well for me. If you do not need your third attention, you had better feel stuck, unhappy, unhealthy, unsatisfied, depressed, turbulent and foggy as possible. Furthermore, you had better make every effort to make bad complexion, bad appetite, bad bowl movement, bad sleeping, bad sex, rough breath happen to you. If you want to suspend your third attention temporarily, you had better eat a little more or smoke or remember unhappy, unhealthy people or stop going to stool or make unpleasant love or not practice any body exercise.

6.You can be conscious of the moment you shoot out your super high speed third attention to a star

When we shoot out our immaterial fibers from our bodies, we can be conscious of shooting out them. The third attention is much subtler and is at much more super high speed than immaterial fiber. It is very difficult for us to be conscious of shooting out the third attention from our bodies. In most cases, we can confirm its existence by the effects which has been brought about by it.

Our third attention can both fly into the far distant universe and bring about any effect within a second or 2 seconds. It is apt to do anything subtly, faintly, swiftly, sweetly, softly, smartly, silently, relentlessly, strongly, perfectly, kindly. Such a way can not be explained by words. The mood of such a way resembles that of the universe and of the spirit. By the way, the universe kills those who do not deserve to enter into them in the same way. The universe heals those who are loved by it in the same way, too.

To be able to confirm the existence of the third attention and handle it, you had better concentrate on your inhalation and exhalation all day everyday for 3 weeks. You will be able to stop your breath automatically. Then, you will be able to lose most of your stickiness and your third attention will appear from your body.

Furthermore, you had better stare at a star which you like for 30 minutes-an hour every night to be able to confirm the existence of your third attention. Your third attention is so fast that it can fly to a 2 billion light year distant star within a second or 2 seconds. The earth is too small for you to be in practice in your third attention. So, it is difficult for you to be conscious of the moment you shoot out it to an object on the earth. But, you can be conscious of the moment you shoot out it to a star. You feel you shoot out something to a star. If you shoot out your third attention to the space between two stars, you feel as if you shot out a gun or cannon shell to the universe from your body.

★ The spirit begins to descend to you while staring at a star

Staring at a star you like, you can be conscious of shooting out your third attention to a star. Your third attention can reach most stars within a second or 2 seconds. You can realize that you can catch on a star. Some day, you may be surprised to find that most stars are like ghosts. They have died and vanished. Only the spinning lights of theirs are flying to the earth. Many kinds of the spirits will descend to you from the places of the universe which you stare at, too. They will descend to you like a big waterfall, shower, powder, falling star, gun, cannon shell, big balloon, soap bubble, cylinder, emptiness, or something. They push or pull you. If you are weak or are not deserved to the spirit, you will be fainted or killed.

Furthermore, you will be apt to carry your thought, voice, feeling, smell, and sense of touch on your third attention to the universe. The spirit floating in the universe finds your offering to the universe, descends to you immediately, and helps you. The noble degree of the spirit descending to you is proportionate to the noble degree of your thought, voice, feeling, smell, sense of touch that you send to the universe.

7. Extreme coldness and extreme hotness of the universe are the origins of the sacred and of power

Most of the universe is in absolute zero (-273.15 c'). Some parts of the universe are in high temperature. Some part of the universe is full of sulfuric acid.

A sticky organism, such as a human being, animal, plant, or devil that lives on the surface of the earth or in inner space, can not live in the harsh environment of the universe. Huna magic in Hawaii says "The meanings for MANA(divine power) are to branch out, and skill and arid, desert", "MA means to fade away, and the syllable NA means calmed, quieted, pacified", "MANA (divine power) was symbolized by water and fire" (Mastering Your Hidden Self by Mr,Serge King). I think water means absolute zero and fire means high temperature in the universe. The harsh universe shuts out sticky organism so that it is sacred and powerful. Your third attention is made from your physical body which is a sticky organism. So, at the beginning, it is difficult for your third attention to break through the sticky warm inner space and enter into the extreme hotness or coldness of the universe. If we fall into a furnace, we will vanish immediately and faint purple smoke will ascent for a split second.

8. To get used to the harsh universe and strengthen your third attention, you have to absorb dry inorganic energy from stones and stars

To get used to the harsh universe and strengthen your third attention not to be killed in the harsh universe, you have to make your third attention absorb dry inorganic energy from stones, stars, the dry inner earth, the dry inorganic spirit and ally as much as possible.

To absorb inorganic energy from a stone, you had better stare at a stone or a rock which you like for 30 minutes-an hour everyday, and put stones around your bed and your house.

I recommend that you put a set of a piece of red granite, a piece of gray granite, a piece of marble, a piece of black-tourmaline on the four corners of your bed or of your body. Ancient Egyptian Pyramids at Giza are made of these four kinds of stones. A coffin in a pyramid is made of red granite. Mr.Edgar Cayce said that a piece of black stone was put on the top of a pyramid and pieces of black stones were sprinkled around the coffin in the pyramid. You had better absorb and feel inorganic energy from these stones around you. You may feel gray granite make you cool. These stones make your stickiness and the fever of depression decrease.

When I attended the Tensegrity workshop in the summer of 1998 in the suburb of Los Angels, I was staring at the rocks of the low mountain every at sunrise and sunset. At the last sunrise, an old dignified strong woman (floating between me and the mountain) appeared saying "You have understood, haven't you?", and gave me dry red energy. When I came back to Japan, I tried to throw up it to the universe from my body. It broke through sticky inner space easily. Furthermore, I could have cleaned up the sky above my house using it, too.

★ A black bird living in Giza Pyramid took me to the white roof of the universe

When my energy body flew to Egypt and entered into the pyramid at Giza for the first time, a black bird appeared in front of me and suddenly flapped violently in the pyramid. This bird took me to the white roof of the universe. I broke through the white roof of the universe 3 years ago. So, it was a second visit to the white roof of the universe. I was peeping at the far distant universe with this bird on the white roof of the universe. The white roof is nothing but the gate of the vast universe. Inner space is the pre-gate of the vast universe. Violent wind was flowing away from the white roof. Since then, this black bird has sometimes appeared in front of me and always flown to the north. I often think I may be destined to fly away into the north of the universe when I vanish into the universe forever.

9. Cut floating sticky pipes to set yourself and other free

Many kinds of sticky, feverish, cold or numb immaterial clouds are floating above our head and our houses. They are running sticky, feverish, cold or numb energy into our bodies so as to weaken or kill us. To set ourselves free or cure diseases of ours or of others', we have to cut the pipe between such a cloud and us. When we can cut a pipe, such a cloud breaks. Then, something like sticky soft excrement suddenly pours down to us or a devil living in such a cloud falls off. Or, to cut such a pipe, we had better spin our bodies stopping the movement of the energy around our bodies. Then, something sticky will spatter once for all violently.

10. Subtle third attention can be compared to a smoke in a treasure-chest. How to handle it?

The third attention is so subtle and faint that it can be compared to a smoke in a treasure-chest. But it is very strong and nimble. An evangelist and pastor, Mr.Mahesh Chavda can handle his subtle and faint third attention. He has All Nations Church in North Carolina in U.S.A. I saw in August, 1999 in Japan that his dry third attention was very strong and could invade into anything immediately although it seemed to be very subtle, faint, weak and light. I could believe that he could revive a dead child in 1985 and cure the 3000 blind at once in Africa.

You had better begin to know the existence of a smoke in a treasure-chest and open a treasure-chest. You have to make a smoke go to any place you want, return to a treasure-chest at any time you want intentionally, and close a treasure-chest. At last, you have to explode a treasure-chest to pieces and make a smoke enter into the universe, never return to the earth forever.

To strengthen and purify a smoke as possible, you have to make a smoke catch on many kinds of the spirits which are more beautiful, drier, glossier, cooler, sweeter, stronger, swifter, nimbler, kinder, softer, more relentless, fiercer. Although the spirits may hate a smoke which tries to catch on the spirits and may try to explode a smoke to death immediately, you have to challenge at your peril to strengthen and purify a smoke (your third attention).

11. The feeling of opposite sex can teach you where to go

If you can not think of the spirit whom you will make your third attention catch on, you had better remember all opposite sexes in detail as much as possible at least 50 times whom you have loved.

You had better remember the color of aura, smell, sense of touch, voice, and temperature of all opposite sexes in detail as possible. You can understand why you have loved. There has been a common denominator which has attracted you. You have lacked the color of aura, smell, sense of touch, voice, and temperature of the common denominator. You need to absorb them to become happier, healthier, and more efficient. So, you had better make your third attention catch on the spirit which has the same energy or atmosphere as that of all opposite sexes' common denominator.

When you can begin to make your third attention venture out to the universe, you may be at a loss where to go. You may feel as if you were like only one salmon at the center of the Pacific. As a salmon returns to the river to have a baby where it was born, you have to enter into some part of the universe where you will be able to become happier, stronger, healthier, more efficient.

To find where to go into the vast universe, you can take advantage of the common denominator about all opposite sexes whom you have loved. At first, you have to be able to enter into the part of the universe which has the same feeling as that of the common denominator about all opposite sexes whom you have loved. If you can do so freely, you don't need opposite sexes on the earth as before. You can begin to make yourself detach from opposite sexes on the earth. Many beautiful angels begin to descend to you at full speed from the universe. You can begin to make friends with these angels who have the same common denominator as that of opposite sexes whom you have loved.

★ Other dirty energy body and devils can break your direction signals

When dirty energy bodies of others' and devils stick to or enter into you, you will become sticky and lose your awareness. They can break your direction signals so that you will become at a loss what to do or how to do or where to go. You will be taken over by them and become unhappy, unhealthy, and inefficient. Then, you had better remember the feeling of the common denominator about all opposite sexes whom you have loved in detail as much as possible to shut out dirty energy bodies of others' and devils. You had better make yourself engulfed by the feeling of the common denominator about all opposite sexes whom you have loved.

★ Opposite sexes are big obstacles and big benefactors for you

In this respect, opposite sexes on the earth are quite strange and odd. They are both big obstacles and big benefactors for us to become psychic astronauts and to become happy, healthy, and efficient. Opposite sexes are like powerful drugs which are both poisons and medicines for us.

We involving me are apt to be egotistic. We can not have forgotten personal indebtedness that other people have incurred to us, but have easily forgotten personal indebtedness that we have incurred to other people. In addition, to square certain personal indebtedness, I imagined good points of all women lively this early morning to whom I have incurred certain personal indebtedness in the course of my life. At the beginning of doing so following the way of "Saying Thank You" in the book-The Active Side of Infinity, I felt as if I opened up an old wound or took a bath of dirty hot water. But, today, I can feel the energy of my sex organ has become stronger and my awareness has become keener than yesterday. I can feel as if I unburdened a certain burden. I can feel happier and more airy. I think we have been badly influenced by the vindictive energy bodies of opposite sexes unconsciously as long as we have neither atoned nor appeased them.

12. Successful people make their third attention work on for them unconsciously, but will be at a loss how to revive it

Happy, healthy, successful people are apt to make their third attention work on for them unconsciously and keep on being happy, healthy, and successful. But, they will be at a loss what to do when they have made their third attention dead and useless. In most cases, they do not know how to revive their third attention. Then, they had better read my book and revive their third attention. They had better remember and recover the feeling of dryness, of rustling, of not getting stuck.

Unhappy, unhealthy, unfortunate people have gotten stuck by stickiness, fever, coldness or numbness, and made their third attention dead and useless. They have not made their third attention work on for them at all, so they can not understand what I have written about the third attention, stickiness, immaterial fiber in my book at all and ignore them.

As for me, I could not have understood the third attention and had ignored it completely if I had not concentrated on my breath everyday for 3 weeks 5 times by 7 years ago and if my third attention had not worked on for me during playing a baseball at the age of 10-11. As a result, I could not have understood Mr, Carlos Castaneda's books, Cabala, Ancient Egyptian Pyramid Text, The Emerald-Tablet of Thoth, Yoga Sutra and so on at all. I think all of them try to teach us how to get rid of stickiness, how to become happy, healthy, efficient, how to be conscious of the third attention, how to handle it, how to contact the spirit, how to fly into the universe freely.

13. To strengthen himself, my young successor (?) will have to fall into heavy oil sea and venture out of it intentionally many times

I have written in Part 2-Astronaut "My young successor (?) looks like a noble fierce hawk and reached Dragon constellation only in 2 seconds".

My young successor (?) is a late teen Brazilian man. He is a bachelor. He will have to experience the origins of complaints, for example, disease and the trouble about opposite sex, children, parents, work, money, or post. These origins of complaints will give my young successor (?) much stickiness. If he can not get rid of much stickiness, he will not be able to venture out to the far distant universe like a noble fierce hawk. In such a case, he will not be able to break through even inner space. So, I have written about him as my young successor(?).

Mr. Carlos Castaneda's book says "One who had a child has had a hole on the surface of one's side. Precious energy begins to leak through a hole". I have a son and 3 daughters. I was much surprised to find a hole 3 inches in diameter on the surface of my left upper side. I can barely have filled up the hole by now.

After my young successor (?) falls into heavy oil sea, survives, and can venture out to the universe, he will be able to become my successor. He will have to go into heavy Oil Sea, and return to the universe intentionally many times.

When his energy body flew to me to Japan all the way from Brazil a year ago, his energy body was touched by a dirty energy body and an unhealthy energy body who was around me. Then, they made his energy body swirl. He seems to have little resistance to a dirty energy body of other's or to an unhealthy energy body of other's. So, he had better strengthen his energy body and his physical body everyday at least in 10 years if he is so crazy as to want to become my successor. He had better do so as earnestly as a first-class man of martial arts does.

14. Like a danger to shut out stickiness

Danger can erase stickiness, too. Domestic animals, pets, garden trees, potted plants, and the crops have much stickiness, but wild animals and wild plants which live in a harsh struggle for existence have little stickiness. So, you had better run a risk at your peril in your life to erase your stickiness.

Sometimes, you had better act desperately about your work and hobby. Sometimes, you had better enter into a dangerous place. Sticky unhealthy-unhappy-inefficient people hate a danger, desperate action, and dangerous place, but rustling healthy-happy-successful people like them and can enjoy them. My young Brazilian successor (?) will have to like a danger and adventure to shut out stickiness, too. Uneducated people are apt to be healthier, happier, or more successful than educated people because uneducated people like a danger and adventure more than educated people do so that they have less stickiness. In this respect, it is very difficult for educated people to become psychic astronauts for lack of enterprise or adventurous spirit.

# Part 5

---

## Body-Response

To become healthy-happy-efficient, follow your body-response to the surroundings. Get rid of poor, flabby, fat, or stiff abdomen, waist, hip, and thigh. This is a founder's way of life. It could cure the trouble of my spine, too. Goethe, the famous German dramatist said "We are tricked not by body-response but by reason"

1. Cure the trouble of my spine, the stiff lamp of my underbelly and my frequent urination by following my body-responses. Buddha taught such a way 2500 years ago
2. Big origin of paralysis, heart disease or cancer is the trouble of spine
3. Stiff lamp of my underbelly and my frequent urination caused by the trouble of my spine could not have been cured by hospitals from the age of 31 until the age of 51. About my impotence and my terrible temper
4. My complaint about my parents had lived in a pouch of sticky bloody pus in the lamp of my underbelly
5. At last, I could find an effective hot spring by following my body-response at the age of 52. Its white energy made my head feel relieved and relaxed
6. Big men of Meiji times revolution had cottages there
7. Sad white energy is useful and obstacle like frost in autumn
8. Ironically my sadness about my father's outrage brought up my psychic ability in my low teens. Clinton. President of U.S.A must have known sadness well
9. I went to Toronto, The Caribbean Sea and Brazil because they had made my body relieved and relaxed
10. How to travel, eat, write, or buy by following my body-response

11. Family live longer happily and big men were raised where my body feels relieved and relaxed. Pastor. Mahesh Chavda has a good power-spot

12. Something like many black army ants ran away from the lamp of my underbelly 3 years ago and I have cured

13. Buddha taught 2500 years ago "Do what your body feel comfortable and your pain will be eliminated". At present, Eugene Gendlin and James Redfield teach the same way

14. Develop the muscles of abdomen, waist, hip, thigh firmly

15. Poor, flabby, fat, or stiff abdomen-waist-hip-thigh can not overcome the surroundings. Women have to strengthen her wombs

16. Don't become like a prizefighter who avoids any fight or hates training. We had better respect both body-exercise and body-response

17. Precisely body-responses have not happened to most of us and are ignored

18. Had better practice Part 1-4 to repair your broken body-response and make friends with founders

19. Test your body-response now! The voice of God?

NEXT Text

1.Cure the trouble of my spine, the stiff lamp of my underbelly and my frequent urination by following my body-responses. Buddha taught such a way 2500 years ago.

The trouble of my spine had tortured me from the age of 31 to the age of 56 because it had kept on causing the stiff lamp of my underbelly and my frequent urination. By following my body-responses obediently, I could have cured them for 4 years since the age of 52. I had ventured to do anything about which my body-response signaled comfortably. They had not been cured by medical treatments and so on at all for long years. I think I should have died of bladder cancer already if I could not have cured them by following my body-response.

Part 5 shows the examples of my body responses. Furthermore, Part 5 is how to cure the trouble of my spine, the stiff lamp of my underbelly and my frequent urination following my body-responses. Buddha taught the same way in India 2500 years ago for us to be able to become healthy, happy and efficient.

2. Big origin of paralysis, heart disease or cancer is the trouble of spine

I think that the first or the second biggest origin of paralysis, heart disease, or cancer is the trouble of spine or the complaint about opposite sex, son, daughter, parent, boss, work, money and post.

Especially, the trouble of spine gives us pangs, internal organ's lump and stiff shoulder. It deprives us of peace, inner silence, joy, happy feeling and efficiency. It always makes us irritated and our blood pressure high. When we quarrel with wife, child, colleague or chief, we fall down easily after the age of 45 because our blood pressure rises up to 180-200 suddenly. At first, we can sit up within 30 seconds-2 hours. In 2-3 years since then, we will fall down completely.

Furthermore, cancer is apt to happen to the internal organ which has lamp. An internal organ is connected with spine through autonomic nerve. So, the internal organ in front of the disordered part of spine begins to become weak, has lamp and cancer is apt to happen to it.

Violent sports (soccer, rugby, and so on), intense exercise, dash, dance, golf, yoga, long meditation, or accident is apt to injure spine.

★ Don't weaken the muscles of the back and abdomen not to turn aside the bone of spine

Furthermore, the weakening of the back's muscle and of abdomen's muscle makes the bone of spine turn aside. Spine is supported by the muscle of the back and of abdomen. When we become older than 50 years old, we are apt to begin to be suffering from the gap of our spine if we have not keep on strengthening the muscle of the back and of abdomen. Stroll (one-hour everyday) and the reverse movement of body (for example, Tensegrity) can strengthen the muscle of the back and of abdomen.

When no problem is with spine, most of us are so careless or so proud of good fortune that most of us say we are too busy to strengthen the muscle of the back and of abdomen. Most of us go anywhere not on foot but by car. Once we begin to be suffering from the trouble of spine, we can not get well easily. The success rate of the operation is not so high. Maybe, we will be half paralyzed as the result of the operation's failure.

3. Stiff lamp of my underbelly and my frequent urination caused by the trouble of my spine could not have been cured by hospitals from the age of 31 until the age of 51. About my impotence and my terrible temper

As I have written in Part 4-Erase stickiness, the complaints about both my parents and my old bitter love trouble had given me much stickiness for 20-34 years. This stickiness had deprived me of joy, peace, ability and made me unhealthy-unhappy-inefficient. Furthermore, my spine was injured by a woman massager of a sauna bath in Tokyo 28 years ago when I was about 31 years old. In those days, I worked for a newspaper as a journalist.

The sauna bath permitted the last customers sleep on the stands of massage until the early morning. My rental apartment was in the suburb of Tokyo. It took me one hour to come back to my apartment from Tokyo. Although I had the wife, I felt tiresome to come back to my apartment when I drank alcohol. After I drank alcohol almost every night, I went to the sauna bath at dead of night and was given a massage. In most cases after a massage, I slept on the stand of massage until the morning. Almost every night, I made a woman massager step my spine.

Then, I tried to get up at my apartment in the morning, but I could not get up because of the pangs of my spine. I could not get up for a week. I felt the pangs whenever I inhaled and exhaled my breath. I felt as if I cried for the pangs of my spine when I went to stool.

A week later, I barely got up and went to Kyoto to cure the gap of my spine. The professional cured the gap of my spine by his fingers and eliminated the pangs of my spine.

But, since then, the subtle unpleasant lamp had happened to my underbelly. It had caused my frequent urination, too. The subtle unpleasant lamp of my underbelly and my frequent urination had kept on torturing me and making me irritated for 25 years.

★ After 1.5 year impotence, I still felt as if an arrow had pierced my underbelly

For one and half a years since then, I had become impotent in spite of the age of 31-32. I could make **with my wife because of conditioned reflex movement (?), but I could make **with other young women by all means. I can remember a young woman teased me about my impotence. She said "Hey, try, try" giving a wry smile. Such impotence had been cured unconsciously.

It is regrettable that the pangs of my spine had happened to me for a week still every year from the age of 31 to the age of 56 when I carried something heavy. The subtle unpleasant lamp of my underbelly and my frequent urination had continued almost everyday persistently, too. I felt as if an arrow or a few thorns had kept on piercing my underbelly or as if I had kept on wearing wet underpants. Furthermore, I had been feeling the hangover of urine. I had urinated too often everyday from the age of 32 to the age of 56.

As I have written in Part 4-Erase stickiness, my third attention has barely begun to work on for me again since the part just above the center of my eyebrows collapsed at the age of 50. But, my third attention worked on for me only when little problem was with my spine, the lamp of my underbelly or my frequent urination.

★ My lamp and frequent urination had made me have a terrible temper

The pangs of my spine could have been eliminated by hanging my body from the instrument for body (hanging for about 2-3 minutes everyday for a week).But, I could have eliminated neither the subtle unpleasant lamp of my underbelly nor my frequent urination for long years. They had made me irritated. They had made me have a terrible temper. I had sometimes lost my temper with my 3 daughters, a son and my wife, and outraged them. I had been neither a good father nor a goodhusband. Thank God, none of my daughters and a son have not become delinquents.

I had been minutely examined at many big hospitals. Nothing had been problem in medical respects. When I insisted on the complaint about my subtle unpleasant lamp of my underbelly and my frequent urination persistently, I was diagnosed with autonomic imbalance. Then, the doctor gave me medicine for autonomic imbalance. I drank it, but it was not effective for me at all.

Acupuncture and moxibustion could cure my subtle unpleasant lamp and my frequent urination only a few days. They relapsed easily. I had tried many folk medicines, but they had not been effective for me at all. Body exercise of yoga, fasting and meditation had been little effective for me, too.

All was lost. I often thought I would pay as much money as possible if some one could cure my unpleasant lamp and my frequent urination.

4. My complaint about my parents had lived in a pouch of sticky bloody pus in the lamp of my underbelly

I have written in Part 4-Erase Stickiness as follows. "When I rented a house in mountains at the age of 45 about 14 years ago, I concentrated only on my breath everyday for 3 weeks. Then, something like a pouch of sticky bloody pus exploded suddenly in my body. A pouch of sticky bloody pus was full of my complaint about my parents. Since then, my complaint about my parents have almost disappeared".

This pouch of sticky bloody pus had been living in the unpleasant lamp of my underbelly. Although the pouch of sticky bloody pus had been eliminated, there had still existed the unpleasant lamp and my frequent urination.

At the age of 51 about 8 years ago, I urinated so often that the crotches of my pants turned to be brown because of my urine leak.I urinated every quarter of an hour and urinated only a little.I took the pants to a laundry, but a laundry could not eliminate the brown of my pants. So, I fired about 20 business suits whose pants turned to be brown heavily in my garden.

Furthermore, the lamp of my underbelly had become stiffer. I felt as if it had been a stone. I often wished I could have gouged the unpleasant lamp of my underbelly by a sharp straight razor. I often felt I would die of bladder-cancer. Because hospitals had been undependable for me, I had not gone to hospital in those days. In those days, the bladder-cancer might have happened to me already.

5. At last, I could find an effective hot spring by following my body-response at the age of 52. Its white energy made my head feel relieved and relaxed

Such a symptom continued for a year. At the age of 52. I took the express train (Sinetu Line of JR) to the back of Japan. When I glanced at the mountain near Karuizawa, the most famous summer resort in Japan, I felt relieved and relaxed again.Whenever I glanced at the mountain through the window of the train since the age of 35, my body felt relieved and relaxed. I wondered why? I looked at the map and could find a hot spring in the mountain whose nearest station is Yokogawa station. So, at last, I got off the train at Karuizawa station, changed the train, and came back to Yokogawa station.

It took me about half an hour to reach a Japanese-style hotel in the hot spring by the hotel's station wagon. The landlord drove the station wagon along a treacherous path which had steep narrow up-slope, many loops and almost perpendicular cliff. I sweated a little with fear and was excited with his dangerous drive. There was only one Japanese-style hotel (Kintokan, TEL Japan 0273-95-3851) in the hot spring almost at the top of the mountain. It had been serviced with electricity recently.

I had a leisurely bath of the hotel. I was submerged up to my neck in the white lukewarm water. I went out of the water and began to wash my body. I drank a few cups of the white lukewarm water, too. It was a marvel that I felt my head became relieved and relaxed while washing my head with the white lukewarm water of the hot spring.

I felt the white lukewarm water was erasing both the stickiness and the fever of depression in my head. Furthermore, I saw a white light began to radiate in my head.

When I came back to my room of the hotel, I looked into my head closing my eyes. The white light was still radiating. I went out of the hotel, I looked down from there at the tops of other mountains. Then, the tops of other mountains radiated white lights, too.

★ White lukewarm water made my lamp twiddled

I stayed one night (about 80 dollars) and came back to my house. Then, I felt the stiff lamp of my underbelly like a stone barely twiddled and became fluid a little. The white lukewarm water decreased the frequency of my frequent urination, too. Hospital, yoga, fasting, meditation, concentrating on my breath, folk medicine had little effect to cure the lamp of my underbelly or my frequent urination, so I was very pleased to find for the first time that a hot spring was effective for them.

Next week, I went to this hot spring again to cure them. I stayed for 2 days on weekdays. I felt my head became relieved and relaxed again while washing my head with the white lukewarm water of the hot spring. I felt the white lukewarm water was erasing both the stickiness and the fever of depression in my head again. Furthermore, I felt a white light radiated in my head .The lamp of my underbelly became more fluid and softer, and the frequency of my frequent urination decreased more.Since then, I had been to this hot spring about 10 times.

6. Big men of Meiji times revolution had cottages there
Only a few or one guest stayed at the hotel weekdays and about 10-20 guests stayed on weekend. I told the landlord"Your hot spring is very

effective for me". I told him " I can feel something special about it". He taught this area was the more famous hot spring and summer resort than Karuizawa about 100 years ago.

Many big men in the revolution of Meiji times (around the turn of the 19th century) and big merchants had their cottages there. Mr. Hirobumi Ito had a cottage there who was a big man in the revolution of Meiji times and the prime minister when Japan won China. All of such cottages had been destroyed by big typhoons because this area was the path of big typhoons. Only this landlord's hotel has been saved. Mr. Kaisyu Katu who was a big man in the revolution of Meiji times often visited the landlord's hotel to cure his piles. His short poem has been engraved on a stone in the hotel's garden.

★ Their tiredness of administering new poor small Japan was erased there

In Meiji times, Japan broke the feudal system and became a modern state. Small poor Japan won big China and big Russia. In those days, it was said "The bigger defect he has, the bigger man he is. A timid sober man is not worthy to talk about". Most ministers of Meiji Government were in twenties. At cabinet councils, most ministers insisted on so violently that they were often on the brink of exchanging blows or flinging chairs.

In the first place, Mr. kaisyu Katu had the vice of making ** with his house's maids one after another, so that his wife said she would not be buried beside his tomb when she died. Mr. Kaisyu Katu often had a narrow escape when he was about to be assassinated by a strong swordsman. Mr. Kaisyu Katu threw away his sword and squatted down cross-legged in front of the strong swordsman saying "Wait, I will be killed by you silently". A strong swordsman could not kill the man who decided to be killed silently without fear. In such a way, he often still had a life. He said "Man should have patience with his bad reputation for 10 years. Disregarding the thoughts of other people, man should do what he believes. 10 years later, other people will change their thoughts and respect such a man". How about Mr. Clinton, President of U.S.A?

There are many hot springs around Tokyo, the capital of Japan. Big men of Meiji times had big power. They could have cottages or villas at any hot spring around Tokyo. Such big men prefer the hot spring in the mountain near Karuizawa (about one and half an hours by express train from Tokyo) and had cottages there because they recognized the special effect of the hot spring's white lukewarm water.

I think their heads must have become relieved and relaxed while washing their heads with the white lukewarm water of the hot spring. I think they felt white lights radiated in their heads. I think the hot spring erased their tiredness that was caused by administering new poor small Japan rivaling other strong big countries.

7. Sad white energy is useful and obstacle like frost in autumn.

If our lungs are healthy and taken over neither by the dirty energy bodies of others nor devils, our lungs can radiate beautiful white lights and shoot out strong white immaterial fibers to catch on an object. Beautiful white energy can cure disease of ours and of others easily, shut out devils, and has strong attack-power like a tiger.

Lung's beautiful white energy is symbolized as tiger, west, west wind, left side of body, 3-5 o'clock in the evening, autumn, moderate sadness, longing, frost, fog, dryness, fastidious women who has craziness, strong intent, power, sadness, and kindness. To bring up beautiful white energy in our bodies, we had better eat fiery foods and strengthen our large intestine and spleen. To strengthen our large intestine, we had better make our bowel movements regular and stimulate the wrist of thumb's root. I think good propolis can make white light twinkle in our bodies, too.

Genius is only one remove from insanity. Lung's beautiful white energy has the character of both genius and insanity. Sadness and longing of lung's white energy can bring up completeness, sobriety and kindness. Sobriety, kindness can bring up wisdom and silent knowledge.

Sadness and longing can make our assemblage points (the core of consciousness) move into the more interior of our bodies than joy. Sadness and longing can strengthen our kidneys. Lung's sadness and longing can bring up the black energy of kidney. The black energy of kidney can give us silent knowledge (voice without voice, silent voice, the voice of God and instinct), patience, detachment, originality and bravery. The Man who has only strength is not a manly man. Man who has both strength and sadness (kindness) is a manly man. Like a manly man, white energy is complex. Goethe, the famous German dramatist (1749-1832) said "Man who has not eaten bread together with tear is not worthy to talk with".

★ Moderate sadness is useful, but too much sadness is poison

To bring up body-response, the immaterial fiber or the third attention which is shot out from our bodies, we have to have 6 kinds of energies which are black energy, blue energy, red energy, transparent energy, yellow energy, and white energy. The lack of one kind of energy or the excess of one kind of energy weakens our body-responses, our immaterial fibers, third attention, health, instinct and ability.

If we have excessive red energy and have not sad white energy, we become too joyful, too active, too ruthless, too sexy, and too lewd. We can not keep ourselves cool, too. We become like plants which do not ripen but flourish. Plants need moderate frost to ripen.

White energy makes us sadden and long until we begin to try and accomplish something that is essential for us to become healthy, happy, and efficient. In such a way, white energy can teach us what to do. White energy is symbolized as frost and our later years. We are apt to feel sad very much in the autumn of our lives. We have to do something by all means to get rid of much sadness and to make ourselves satisfied. If we don't do so, we will be killed by too much sadness. Crops can not ripen in the autumn if there is a heavy frost.

Sadness is strange and odd. It is useful and obstacle for us. It is like powerful drugs.

8. Ironically my sadness about my father's outrage brought up my psychic ability in my low teens. Clinton, the president of U.S.A has known sadness well

Mr. Clinton, the president of U.S.A has much white and green energy in his body, so I think he has experienced and known sadness well. I had often been outraged by my father so violently in my hometown house that the bone of my left wrist was broken.

When I was knocked down or kicked by my father in my early teens, I ran away from my hometown house, felt sad and wept somewhere for 1-2 hours. Then, I always began to feel relieved and relaxed. I could feel peculiar inner silence. I felt as if a cave had opened in my abdomen. Much energy ascended my central energy pipe. I was engulfed by white energy. I could see that my father regretted deeply to outrage me. It was the moment that body-response happened to me and my assemblage point was moved into the interior of my body by sadness so that I could shoot out my immaterial fiber or third attention to my father and see him.

Sadness, fear, deep anger against my father could move my assemblage point into the interior of my bodies than joy. I think it made me see an ally (inorganic-being who has given me the ability to fly into the far distant universe) twice and made my third attention work on for me for the first time while playing baseball as a pitcher early in my teens (they are written in Part 4-Erase Stickiness).

In addition, I often tried to leap up and float in the air like a ninja in my childhood. I often played as a ninja with one of my friends. I could not float in the air, but the back of my foot, my foot and my calf could feel the repulsion-power of the earth for a split second while leaping up. Feeling the repulsion-power of the earth made me funny very much and made me leap up again and again everyday. I think it could make my assemblage point move into the interior of my bodies and brought up my psychic ability, too. I think now it made me meet an ally at night and gave me silent knowledge (voice without voice) while playing baseball in my childhood, too. It is effective to strengthen your internal organs or attain the supernatural power that you make the back of your foot, your foot and your calf feel the repulsion-power and the gravity of the earth everyday for a few years. In such a way, the earth can give you a big present such as happy lucky feeling, solace and power to withstand strong black energy (called Eagle in Mr. Carlos Castaneda's books) and can teach you the path to the universe or a phenix.

9. I went to Toronto, Caribbean Sea and Brazil because they had made my body relieved and relaxed

Since the hot spring of white lukewarm water made me feel relieved, relaxed and began to cure the lamp of my underbelly and my frequent urination at the age of 51, I have begun to follow the comfortable response of my body to my surroundings. I have tried to awake comfortable or uncomfortable response of my body as possible before I go, eat, buy, meet, drink, listen, or write. If I awake a comfortable response of my body, I will go, eat, buy, meet, drink, listen or write.

I went to Toronto in Canada that is at the bank of Lake Ontario 5 years ago because I felt relieved when I uttered the word "Toronto" a few times. The cool clear transparent atmosphere of Toronto made me relieved and relaxed when I visited Toronto. Furthermore, I felt relieved and relaxed while I was looking into the water of Lake Ontario. In spite of the fairly dirty water, I was not weary of looking into it. I entered into the water and watered my head. My head felt relieved and became clear. The stickiness and depression's fever of my head were erased by the water of Lake Ontario. I felt that much white energy was ascending from Lake Ontario.

★ Caribbean Sea has healthy pulse, surface tension, elasticity and green energy

Whenever I imagined The Caribbean Sea, I felt comfortable. Furthermore, the stiff lamp of my underbelly became fluid and soft. I could find my abdomen relaxed and pleased. I often enlarged my energy body to the size of a giant and made my energy body play in The Caribbean Sea as if it were a bath. So, I visited and swum in the Caribbean Sea 5 years ago after I attended the conference at The University of Wisconsin. Although I was looking at The Caribbean Sea practically for long hours, I did not lose interest in it.

I felt strong healthy pulse, surface tension, elasticity, and green energy in The Caribbean Sea. I felt as if it were a living thing. Whenever I remember the feeling of The Caribbean Sea in Japan, the lamp of my underbelly and my frequent urination got well little by little.

★ Sweet water and firing earth of Amazon has changed my constitution

In December, 1995, I stayed Amazon in Brazil about for 3 weeks. My head felt relieved whenever I took a shower in Rio de Janeiro in Brazil in the summer of 1995. So, I visited Brazil again in December, 1995 and went to the jungle region of Amazon.

The water of water service in Amazon region was yellow and sweet. It emitted the smell of mud and of sand. Whenever I took a shower and drank it, I felt relieved and relaxed. After I kept on drinking the water of Amazon, the smell of my excrement and of urine became the same smell as that of Amazon's water. Furthermore, I felt as if the region's earth between Rio Branco and Boca do Acre had been firing 10 feet in height. I felt as if the fire of Amazon's earth had burned the dirty sticky energy of my abdomen. The water and earth of Amazon has changed my constitution and made my character franker.

Some Brazil musics which Mr. R, my Brazilian friend selected from his radio could erase the stickiness of my body's central energy pipe. When I began to listen to these musics, I could feel that tickle happened at the top of my head and energy began to circulate between my head and my abdomen. The sound of these musics was light and heavy, weak and strong, noble and fierce, lovely and fearful, sexy and sober, sweet and ruthless, peaceful and nimble, cool and passionate. It can not be explained by the words on the earth. Its atmosphere was the same as those of the far distant universe and of the Holy Spirit. In return, I presented the ability of psychic ear to this Brazilian friend.

10. How to travel, eat, write, or buy by following my body-response
I have been to Tyousi about 10 times since 4 years ago which is a famous fishing harbor 2 hours distant by car from my house. When I wondered if I went to Tyousi, I felt relieved. So, I went to Tyousi and ate raw fish at a cheap restaurant. Then, I felt more relieved. The lamp of my underbelly and my frequent urination got well more.

Furthermore, I have eaten or drunken the products grown at the region which I feel relieved or comfortable. So, I have kept on eating the rice of Akita prefecture in Japan, and sometimes drink vodka of Russia.

I wrote a fourth book in Japanese with the title-How to concentrate on your breath and stop it automatically 7 years ago because energy ascended from my abdomen while gathering material (in Chinese) for the book. I felt as if I had been burning while reading Chinese material, so I decided to write about it.

When I have to buy new color TV, air conditioner, refrigerator and so on, I stand in front of them and try to feel my body-response silently. When my body can feel relieved and relaxed about them, I will buy them.

11. Family live longer happily and big men were raised where my body feel relieved and relaxed. Pastor, Mahesh Chavda has a good power-spot
When I stay at a Japanese-style hotel, I will stay at a hotel about which my body feels relieved and relaxed in front of a hotel. When my body feels relieved and relaxed in front of a hotel, most landlords' family live longer and happier. Three generations of landlord often live together happier in the hotel. As soon as I enter a hotel, I often ask landlord or his wife "Your family live longer happily, don't you?". Then, I am always asked "That is

right. Why do you know?". The hotel is at a power-spot whose energy is beautiful, dry, and glossy.

An evangelist and pastor, Mr. Mahesh Chavda said in August, 1999 in Japan "Since I moved from Florida, my many followers have begun to be fainted or drunken by the spirit in my church, All Nations Church in North Carolina in U.S.A. Many lights can been seen in my church, too. Many people have begun to come to our all-night Friday prayers from all over the country by sightseeing buses". I think it is because that he has rebuilt his church at a power-spot in North Carolina.

I can have confirmed big men were raised in the house at a power-spot whose energy is not dirty, sticky, feverish, cold or numb, too. All big men have cleaned-up central energy pipes in their body. Their central energy pipes don't get stuck. All big men are not like twisty cucumbers. Their voices are uttered not from their mouths but from the central energy pipes of their bodies. When I visit a big man's house, my central energy pipe becomes less stuck and less sticky. I try to find the best power-spot in a big man's house and I sit down or stand there.

★ Turned out a big flat snake from my hometown house's garden

So, from Tokyo I saw my hometown house and garden in Kyoto prefecture 2 years ago because former 3 generations of my family had been unhappy. Then, I could find that my hometown house and the garden had been taken over by black and gray dirty sticky energy which was a foot in thickness. This energy moved like a big flat snake. The Active Side of Infinity which is published 2 years ago explains it as a mud shadow. I cleaned up the sky, surface and ground of my hometown house. When I came back to my hometown house a year ago, I was surprised to see beautiful white energy ascended to the sky from the window of my hometown house's ceiling.

12. Something like many black army ants ran away from the lamp of my underbelly 3 years ago and I have cured

Don Juan Matus says in the book, Tales of Power "Power always makes a cubic centimeter of chance available to a warrior. The warrior's art is to be perennially fluid in order to pluck it".

Useful power, devil, dirty energy body of other, or floating dirty sticky cloud sticks a pipe into our physical bodies or energy bodies while we are dreaming at night or moving in the daytime. We have to pluck or enter a

pipe of useful power which is beautiful, dry, glossy, cool, active, of abandon, of largesse, and of humor. I have begun to find the hole of such a
pipe's tip in the sky while dreaming since 3 years ago. I have approached
it and entered into it while dreaming. After going through such a pipe,
there exist beautiful another world which is 2-4 km in diameter.

A third time I tried to go through such a pipe 3 years ago, it was broken. Suddenly something like an exhausted snake ran away from my
central energy pipe. Furthermore, something like 20-30 tenacious strong
black army ants ran away from the lamp of my underbelly. Since then, the
lamp of my underbelly, my frequent urination and the trouble of my spine
have been cured. They had been torturing me for 25 years since my spine
was injured at the age of 31 by a massager woman.

In spite of the complete recovery, I have been so careful that I have still
kept on taking an hour stroll and practicing the reverse movement of my
body everyday in order to strengthen the muscle of the back and of my
abdomen. It has prevented the bone of my spine from turning aside.

13. Buddha taught 2500 years ago "Do what your body feel comfortable
and your pain will be eliminated". At present, Eugene Gendlin, James
Redfield teach the same way

There have been hundreds of body exercises, yoga, meditation, prays,
mantra, stares, breath's way, and fasting. Many various practices are written in Carlos Castaneda's books, too. If we test for 2-3 months per way,
we can not finish testing the ways of all practices by we pass away. I have
begun to practice them since the age of 37. Especially from age of 45 until
the age of 51, I had been practicing them for 7-8 hours everyday. Then,
at last I felt as if I had been imprisoned and felt sad.

Buddha had been practicing many ways involving fasting crazily for 6
years 2500 years ago and stopped practicing them at the age of 35. He
taught his followers (1) the origin of pain is not following comfortable
body's response (2) don't do what your body feel uncomfortable (3) what
your body feel comfortable is accurate (4) do what your body feel comfortable and your pain will be eliminated.

At present Mr. Eugene T Gendlin teaches the same way in the book
with the title-Focusing. Mr. James Redfield and Carol Adrienne introduces
the same way in the book with the title-The Celestine Prophecy, too.

I had cured the lamp of my underbelly, my frequent urination and the trouble of my spine by the grace of following my body's responses. Whenever I glanced at the mountain near Karuizawa through a window of a train, my head felt relieved and relaxed. That is to say, my body tried to teach me what to do to cure the lamp of my underbelly, my frequent urination and the trouble of my spine as the above mentioned sentence.

If I had been stupid or donkey enough to ignore such a body's response to the end, I might have died of bladder cancer already.

★ Examples of body-responses

Don Juan Matus taught such body responses to his disciple, the late Mr. Carlos Castaneda (1) tickle happens at the top of head and descends to the back, waist, and womb (in such a case, assemblage point moves into the interior of the body and can feel accurate decision making or judgment without an illusion) (2) see the Nagual (the subtle third attention or the spirit) (3) see the immaterial fiber of the universe (4) sound happens in the recess of throat as if a wooden pipe were snapped (5) feel as if a cave opened in the abdomen and energy ascends from the abdomen (6) overwhelming premonition (7) can hear the voice without uttering on the back of ear (8) feel as if we could perceive about two places or exist at two places simultaneously.

Don Juan Matus says that in these cases we can shoot out the immaterial fiber or our subtle third attention to an outside object from our bodies and can judge it accurately.

Mr. Eugene T Gendlin introduces body-responses in his book with the title-Focusing: (9) we begin to feel relieved and relaxed (10) begin to take a deep breath (11) stiff abdomen turns to be fluid and relaxed. Mr. James Redfield and Carol Adrienne introduce body-response in their book with the title-The Celestine Prophecy: (12)"We feel beautiful, relieved or relaxed when we see or visit someone, something, some place which can give us something useful".

Some executive says in the book with the title-Executive ESP: (13) "When I have made an accurate decision, I feel a click".

14. Develop the muscles of abdomen, waist, hip, thigh firmly

By practicing contents of Part 1-4, we have to make our appearances changed. To bring up or strengthen our body-responses, our immaterial fibers and our third attention, we have to develop the muscles of abdomen, waist, hip, and thigh firmly. We have to be able to petrify the muscle of abdomen like steel and soften it like water intentionally. Needless to say, good complexion and rejuvenation (grow at least 10-20 years younger) have to happen to us, too.

I can see that don Juan Matus and don Genaro had developed the muscles of abdomen, waist, hip, thigh firmly more than don Juan Matus' teacher.Julian Osario. So, they are more powerful, can see through more and can be floating in the more upper universe than Julian Osario. I have not sufficiently developed these muscles firmly because I had been tortured for long years by the trouble of my spine, the lamp of my underbelly and my frequent urination. It is my weak point that I will have to overcome by all means.

15. Poor, flabby, fat, or stiff abdomen-waist-hip-thigh can not overcome the surroundings. Women have to strengthen her wombs

The late Mr. Mihara, the famous baseball manager in Japan had fired the baseball player who had lost the muscles of his hip and of his waist. Whenever Mr. Mihara wondered if some player of his team was fired, he entered a public bath with the player and peeped at the muscles of the player's hip and of the player's waist.

In this respect, most of us, most pastors and most psychic teachers are apt to have the bad muscles (poor, flabby, fat or stiff) of abdomen, waist, hip, thigh because most of us and they are apt to go anywhere not on foot but by car. Most of us and they are apt to practice no body-exercise at all and eat too much, too. Most executives and elite seem to have the same inclination and apt to be disgraced miserably sooner or later. Needless to say, women have to strengthen her wombs.

★ Christianity had better make a point of body-exercise or sports

I think Christ and Buddha did not teach " we have to make a point of body exercise or sports to become healthy-happy-efficient" to us 2000-2500 years ago. I think it is right because people in those days had to walk and work without cars or machines. They moved their bodies well everyday and did not need more stroll, body-exercise, or sports than at present. To the contrary, at present most of us, most pastors, most psychic teachers, most executive and elite are apt to need more stroll, body-exercise or sports everyday than long years ago because of cars, machines or too much eating.

Only praying, reading doctrines, singing, meditation and worrying about management everyday are apt to weaken their bodies and hearts easily. To survive and prosper at present, Christianity and Buddhism had better change their doctrines according to the change of our society.

16. Don't become like a prizefighter who avoids any fight or hates training. We had better make a point of both body-exercise and body-response

What I have written in Part 1-4 can be compared to <1>a shadow-boxing <2> entering the hospital of psychiatrist for treatment <3>or a maintenance garage for broken fighters.

If we respect only what I have written in Part 1-4 (body exercise, sports, stroll, moderation of life, standard weight, no smoking, fast, saving sex energy, concentrating breath, body exercise of yoga, stare, body-exercise of Chinese martial arts, making friends with danger) and ignore what I have written in Part 5 (respect body-responses and follow them), we will be compared to (1) prizefighters avoiding any fight (2) strange men(or women)not leaving the hospital of psychiatrist although they almost have gotten well (3) or fighters abandoned in a maintenance garage although their radars and guided missiles have been repaired.

If we respect only what I have written in part 5 and ignore what I have written in Part 1-4, we will be compared to (4) prizefighters hating training (5) mental patients avoiding entering the hospital of psychiatrist (6) or fighters flying without repairing their broken radars or guided missiles.

We can not become strong prizefighters without long hard training. On the contrary, if we practice only training and avoid any fight, we will become timid and become like a rotten apple. If we fight and are beaten, we only study why to be beaten and strengthen ourselves through training. If we are so proud of our strength as to hate training after we become strong prizefighters, we will be beaten deadly sooner or later. So, I think we had better respect both what I have written in Part 1-4 and what I have written in Part 5 (Body-Response).

17. Precisely body-responses have not happened to most of us and are ignored

Precisely, above-mentioned body-responses have not happened to most of us at all. Furthermore, most of us ignore them because of no good reason to believe if body-responses happen to them by any chance.

Dirty energy bodies of others, devils and our complaints have given most of us much stickiness, depression's fever, coldness or numbness. The complaints about health, opposite sex, son, daughter, parents, boss, work, money or post can give us much bad energy. This much bad stickiness, depression's fever, coldness or numbness has broken the direction signals of our bodies. So, body-response has not worked on for us.

Furthermore, we have not been taught to respect or follow body-responses in schools or companies. We have been taught to ignore them there. We have been taught to respect and follow plausible reasons. For example, we have been taught to believe in the prospects of stock prices that have plausible reasons. Most of us ignore body-responses if they happen to most of us.

18. Had better practice Part 1-4 to repair your broken body-response and make friends with founders

In most cases, to repair the direction signals of our bodies and make body-responses work on for us, we had better practice what I have written in Part 1-4. After good complexion, rejuvenation, good appetite, good sleeping, good bowel movement, soft shoulder, happy feeling, subtle breath, dryness, and gloss begin to happen to us little by little, body-responses are apt to happen to us little by little. That is to say, body-responses will happen to us little by little after we begin to have good complexion, begin to develop the muscles of abdomen, waist, hip, thigh firmly, and begin to get rid of poor, flabby, fat, or stiff abdomen-waist-hip-thigh by practicing what I have written in Part 1-4.

If body-responses begin to happen to us, we had better run a risk to follow them at our perils. If we are so timid that we can not follow them, we had better follow the body-response to our hobbies, eating, furniture and something that don't need much money. At least, we can respect and follow the body-responses to our private lives as much as possible.

Successful founders in various channels, enterprisers and pioneers are apt to ignore plausible reasons, respect and venture to follow their body-responses. They are often uneducated people. They have not been poisoned by education. So, we had better make friends with them to imitate such features.

19. Test your body-response now! The voice of God?

First of all, you had better test your body-response to my book with the help of Part 5-Body-Response. How about your body-response to my book just before you begin to read it? The scripture says " Like a baby, you had better thirst for the voice of God". The voice of God is one of the body-responses. It is a voice without uttering on the back of your ear. Can you hear such a voice about my book just before you begin to read my book? The voice of God(the voice without voice, silent voice, silent knowledge, and the ascent of your kidney's black energy) ascends from your abdomen to the back of your left ear. Or, can your body feel comfortable or uncomfortable about my book just before you begin to read it or while reading it? Can your body feel the color, smell, touch's sense, sound or flavor of my book? In addition, can you see my face through my book? Can your body feel the color, smell, touch's sense, sound or flavor of my body?

Please, estimate my book not by plausible reasons but by your body-response. Goethe, the famous German dramatist said "we are tricked not by body-responses but by reason". If no body-response happens to you at all, you had better realize that your body-response has been broken. So, you had better enter a training gym, hospital of psychiatrist or maintenance garage for a while (at least 3 years).

In most cases, if you remember your life in detail at least 50 times, you will realize that you have tried to do new many things and chase men or women one after another ignoring your body-response or not waiting body-response and failed one after another. So, don Juan Matus says "It is dangerous and vain for us to act before comfortable body-response happens to us".

# Part 6

## Good Feeling

The Scriptures say "Kingdom is coming. Repent!". Repent is to change your bad feeling. Happy good feeling is power. Happy good feeling can give you a supernatural power, cure diseases and change your surroundings for better. Happy good feeling is proportionate to the degree of your internal organ's strength and of the ability to stop your breath automatically. For example, fasting is effective to strengthen your internal organs. By the way, I have unveiled the dangerous white gate of heaven for the first time.

1. Test how much power and good feeling you have now. You will be sent a present when you think about someone?

2. Don Juan Matus says "Power is a lucky feeling. You should deepen four kinds of good feelings as possible"

3. The lively you can imagine good feeling, the more easily you can change your dream and surroundings

4. The ability to imagine good feeling is proportionate to your healthy strong internal organs and the ability to stop your breath automatically

5. Healthy strong liver gives you the feeling of light spring breeze or of a tree's sprout which can relax and seduce other people

6. Healthy strong heart gives you the feeling of self-confidence and of joy which can cure disease and swallow up an outside object

7. A white stone image of Buddha has given me a piece of burning stone table and a piece of cool black gray stone table. Joyful red energy of heart has to be cooled by cool white foggy energy of lung

8. Some woman's energy body exploded to pieces and was sucked into the white world (heaven, the white spirit's world). So, I gathered up the pieces and hardened them into her former body

9. An owner of a stock farm in Brazil could come back to the earth from Venus by remembering her womb lively

10. To break through the dangerous white gate of heaven without being killed, you had better temper yourself

11. An offensive ally took me to the tip of some vast flying black universe

12. I was overwhelmed by an unbending, unwavering strong intent of some vast flying black universe's tip which is rushing headlong. I often remember its feeling lively to recover

13. We need both light, glossy, sweet feeling and self-confident, brave feeling of insane genius. If you have not a well-balanced feeling, you will be disgraced by many attacks of others or be looked down upon

14. The Scriptures say "The Kingdom (heaven, the spirit) is coming to you. Repent!". The etymology of "Repent!" is to change your bad feeling

NEXT Text

1.Test how much power and good feeling you have now. You will be sent a present when you think about someone?

Please, test how much power and good feeling you have now before you begin to read Part 6. Test (1) when you think about a good point of someone (who is at a different place) for a few seconds-30 minutes, someone will send you a present, invite you to dinner or call you in 3 days although you do not ask someone to do so (2) when you think about a good point of someone (who is at a different place) for a few seconds-30 minutes, someone will recover from the serious illness or will get well (3) when you stare at a stray cat, it will suddenly lies on its back in front of you and show its abdomen to show you honor.

If none of them happens to you, you have neither power nor happy good feeling at all. You have to recognize "I have given poison to someone and a stray cat, or can have given nothing to them. I am unhealthy-unhappy-inefficient now". In such a case, please, read this book many times and recover power and happy good feeling. If you are a big man or founder or enterpriser, you had better retire amicably before you are miserably disgraced.

If two thirds of (1)(2)(3) or all (1)(2)(3) happen to you, You have power and happy good feeling. You have to recognize "I have given something good to someone or a stray cat. I am healthy-happy-efficient". In such a case, you do not have to read this book or had better read it once to prepare against the future loss of your power and of your happy good feeling. If you are a big man, founder or enterpriser, you do not have to retire and had better be active in the front lines. If you are so crazy as to want to become a psychic astronaut, you have the hidden ability to become a psychic astronaut. In such a case, you had better read my book many times and keep on multiplying your power and your happy good feeling at least for 10 years.

2. Don Juan Matus says "Power is a lucky feeling. You should deepen four kinds of good feelings as possible"

I have written in Part 5-Body-Response "To become healthy-happy-efficient, follow your body-response to your surroundings. Goethe said that we are tricked not by body-response but by reason ". But, body-response has not happened to most of us because it has been broken by our stickiness, complaints, lack of body-exercise, bad abdomens-hips and so on. So, most of us can neither find nor catch what gives health-happiness-efficiency to us. What can give health-happiness-efficiency to us is power. Power is special good feeling, mood, atmosphere, another world and time.

Most of us have been confined to the bad feeling which is sticky, feverish, cold, numb, anger, hate, irritated, self-pity, guilty, fearful, gloomy, dull, cynical, stubborn, restless, busy, sly, and timid. Such a feeling is the core of unhealthy-unhappy-inefficient individual and home. That is to say, in such a case, our immaterial fibers or third attention are confined to dirty energy (something like heavy oil, sludge, mud, sewage) of our bodies and can not be shot out of our bodies to an outside object. We can not see an outside object through accurately and can neither control nor change it freely. If we are confined to such a bad feeling for long time, we will made our immaterial fibers or third attention almost dead and will become unhealthy-unhappy-inefficient. Unfortunately, we will have forgotten another special good feeling if we have been confined to the bad feeling for long time, at least half a year.

★ To break from bad feeling, you had better imagine a good point of each season lively

To break from the bad feeling, you had better remember (1) the common denominators about all opposite sexes whom you have loved (aura's color, smell, sense of touch, voice, temperature of all opposite sexes in detail as possible whom you have loved) (2) the happiest scene in your life.

Furthermore, to break from the bad feeling, you had better imagine (3) the spring, east wind in the morning, light spring breeze, morning, sprout, adolescence, young virgin, the right side of body, healthy strong liver, healthy strong tendon, good eye, cunning, blue color, primeval tree, rancid smell, twitter, being airy and nimble(4) the summer, south wind at night, daytime, luxuriance, youth, the back of body, healthy strong heart, smell of burning, joy, ruthless, sex appeal, lewdness, activity, grow thick, catch on, swallow up, self-confidence, taking care of somebody, red, fire, riotousness (5) the end of summer, southwest wind in the end of summer, at P.M 2-3, manhood, healthy strong spleen, healthy strong muscle, sweet, yellow, the center of the earth, hidden super-power, hidden big collapse, hidden super phenix, fragrant smell, chemical reaction, digestion, change ,invasion and adhering, peace (6) the autumn, purification, west wind in the autumn, at P.M 3-5, the beginning of late life, the left side of body, healthy strong lung, healthy beautiful skin, ripeness, beautiful white color, frost, tiger, choose, the sky of autumn, fishing smell, moderate sadness, genius and insanity, strictness (7) transparency, healthy strong V-spot on the crest of the sternum at the base of your neck, clarity, smooth, seer, the eye of hawk(8) the winter, north wind in winter, at noon, late life, the front of body, healthy strong kidney, healthy strong bones, good ear, stop, death, rest, detachment, black, mother, water, silent voice on the back of the ear, decree, rotten smell, patience, bravery, rushing headlong, originality, arrogance.

You had better make yourself engulfed by each feeling,too.

Don Juan Matus, the teacher of the late Mr.Carlos Castaneda says in the book with the title-Journey to Ixtlan "Personal power is a feeling. Something like being lucky. Or one may call it a mood", in the book with the title-Power of Silence "You need to be ruthless (like the summer), cunning (like the spring), patient (like the winter) and sweet (like the summer end). Ruthlessness should not be harshness, cunning should not be cruelty, patience should not be negligence, sweetness should not be foolishness".

If you have been confined to the bad feeling for long years (or for several months) and forgotten another special good feeling completely, you had better imagine your bad feeling at the beginning and (1)->(2)->(3)->(4)->(5)->(6)->(7)->(8)->your bad feeling one after another. Then, you can find the best feeling of these feelings which you have imagined and can begin to keep on having the best feeling of these feelings that you have imagined.

3. The lively you can imagine good feeling, the more easily you can change your dream and surroundings

The lively you can imagine so, the more easily you can begin to change your dream during dreaming intentionally. The lively you can imagine so, the more easily you can change your surroundings. After you can change your dream during dreaming intentionally, you will begin to change your surroundings. For example, someone around you feels cold in the summer when you imagine the coldness of the winter in spite of being in the summer. If you can imagine the feeling of the summer's rain lively in the dry season, it will begin to rain in the dry season. You had better be able to change the scenes during dreaming intentionally, too. As a result, you can cure your or other disease and can improve your surroundings by imagining good feeling. Furthermore, an angel or the spirit that has the same feeling as your good feeling begins to approach you and help you after you threw away bad feelings and begin to have new good feeling. So, you will cure disease and improve your surroundings much more easily.

★ Grasp both the tip of the spirit's pipe and its pipe

The spirit that is floating in the universe, inner space, the interior of the earth is approaching as a gassy energy of special color or a transparent energy. If you can see that the spirit of good feeling is approaching you, you had better make your immaterial fiber or third attention catch on it.

The spirit sticks its pipe into your physical body or your energy body while dreaming, too. In such a case, you had better grasp both the tip of the pipe and the pipe in your dream if you feel better about the feeling of its tip. You can keep on grasping the spirit for longer time than you grasp only its tip. At A.M 3 yesterday, I was aware that the tip of the spirit's pipe stuck in my right eye and flashed in my dream. It had a healthy strong feeling of white and red color. It seemed to have the ability to erase stickiness or the fever of depression in our bodies. It seemed that I would be able to cure diseases of others by flowing it to others. Its scene was very lively. I thought its scene was not an illusion but a reality. So, I got up immediately, went out of my house, and looked up the sky from which the spirit seemed to shoot out a pipe to me. Then, the flashing energy of good feeling descended to me from the sky. I was presented a new different good feeling last night by the spirit, too.

4. The ability to imagine good feeling is proportionate to your healthy strong internal organs and the ability to stop your breath automatically

Imaging good feelings is compared to putting key word into a personal computer. The ability to imagine good feelings is proportionate to the beauty, dryness, gloss, flexibility, activity, and peace of your energy body. These of your energy body are proportionate to your good complexion, rejuvenation, good appetite, good sleeping, good bowel movement, and soft shoulder. These healthy features are proportionate to (1) healthy strong liver-gallbladder, healthy strong heart-a small intestine, a pancreas, the healthy strong spleen-stomach, healthy strong lung-a large intestine, healthy strong V-spot of neck, healthy strong kidney-bladder (2) developing the muscles of abdomen, waist, hip, thigh firmly (getting rid of poor, flabby, fat, or stiff abdomen, waist, hip, thigh) (3) having good spine (4) shutting out opposite sexes without sadness, or making pleasant and satisfied * * with opposite sexes(5) the ability to stop your breath automatically (6) eating in moderation.

(1)(2)(3)(4)(5)are proportionate to practicing what I have written in my Part 1-4 (body exercise, moderation of life, stroll, not smoking, standard weight, yoga, saving sex energy, concentrating on breath, fasting, stare, body exercise of Chinese martial arts, making friends with danger) and what I have written in Part 5-Body-response.

★ Take your personal computer from sludge and repair

Whenever you listen to a lecture of psychology, religion or management, you may be taught many times "You will be healthy-successful if you have a positive thinking and positive self-image". But, in most cases, you will fail to have a positive thinking and positive self-image and fail to realize health and success whenever you try to have such a thinking and self-image.

It is because that dirty energy body of other, devil and complaints (about opposite sex, health, son or daughter, parents, boss, money, work, and post) have made your energy body dirty, sticky, feverish, cold or numb. As a result, the ability to imagine positive thinking and positive self-image has declined.

It can be compared to putting the key word (positive thinking and positive self-image) into a personal computer which has fallen into heavy oil, sludge or sewage. You had better take the personal computer from heavy oil, sludge, sewage, and wash->repair-> make it run on electricity. Then, you can put the key word into it and make it work on for you. What I have written in Part 1-5 is compared to taking such a personal computer from heavy oil, sludge, sewage and washing->repairing->making it run on electricity again. So, practicing what I have written in Part 1-5, you had better imagine above-mentioned good feelings,

★ Healthy internal organs can give you good feeling, so you had better strengthen them

Healthy strong liver can give you the good feeling of the spring and of light spring breeze. Healthy strong heart can give you the good feeling of the summer, of joy, and of self-confidence. Healthy strong spleen can give you the good feeling of the late summer, of peace and of love. Healthy strong lung can give you the good feeling of the autumn, of moderate sadness, of purification. Healthy strong V-spot of neck can give you the good feeling of transparence and of seer. Healthy strong kidney can give you the good feeling of the winter, of bravery and of originality.

So, you had better cure or strengthen your liver, heart, spleen, lung, V-spot, and kidney by all means, for example by what I have written in Part 1-5. There exist close connections through energy pipes between liver and gallbladder, between heart and a small intestine-pancreas, between spleen and stomach, between lung and a large intestine, between kidney and bladder. As a result, to cure or strengthen your liver, heart, spleen, lung, and kidney, you had better cure or strengthen your gallbladder, a small intestine-pancreas, stomach, a large intestine and bladder, too.

5. Healthy strong liver gives you the feeling of light spring breeze or of a tree's sprout which can relax and seduce other people

If you have cured or strengthen your liver, you can enjoy the same good feeling as that of light spring breeze, of a tree's sprout or of an innocent adolescent. Most of us have thrown away such a feeling since most of us begin to have the trouble of spine or some complaints about opposite sex, health, son or daughter, parents, boss, money, work or post. I had forgotten such a feeling for about 40 years, too. Sometimes, I can have begun to enjoy such a feeling since 2 years ago. I feel as if light spring breeze skimmed through my body. Then, I am engulfed by beautiful blue or green energy. I feel as if I have revived.

Blue energy is like the feeling of light spring breeze, of a tree's sprout or of an innocent adolescent. Blue energy has a special power. It seems to be weak at first, but it is really strong. It can make others relaxed and revived. It has a peculiar pheromone. It can disarm anybody without orders or threat, and can use anybody freely without order or money. Anybody is apt to follow it voluntarily. It is apt to gain, use, and control anybody or anything without endeavor to do so.

Most of us have thrown away such a peculiar pheromone and become cynical since a big lost love and divorce, but big men have not done so

Most of us have thrown away such a strange energy after most of us lost a big love, were divorced, betrayed, beaten, or failed in something. If we have thrown away it, we will become like machines without lubricant. We will lose cunning and smooth. Unhappy-unhealthy-inefficient people lack in such a strange blue energy. As a result, they will become dull, tired, or irritated. They will lack in sex energy which has a close connection with liver. They can make ** with opposite sex only once or twice a month even if they want to do so more times. They may have a terrible temper, too. They think "I can not believe other people. I have to depend upon only myself". They become cynical. Then, they become like inefficient machines without lubricant, so that they will not be able to neither believe other people nor depend upon themselves after all. They will be able to believe neither other people nor themselves, so that they will become more cynical and will not recover light spring breeze's feeling of blue energy for long years or forever.

Happy-healthy-efficient people or big men have such a strange energy more or less which seduce other people. So, we have to endeavor not to throw away such a strange blue energy even when we fail in something.

I flow such a strange blue energy to someone in secret when I am full of such a strange blue energy. Then, someone will send me a present or call to invite me even though I do not ask to do so.

★ Keep up with innocent low teens and healthy young virgin

To strengthen liver and increase beautiful blue energy, imagining light spring breeze's feeling of beautiful strong blue energy, fasting, becoming a vegetarian as possible and good bowl movement are the most effective in what I have written in Part 6 and Part 1-4. Needless to say, we have to stop drinking alcohol too much. Eating acid foods, keeping up with innocent low teens or healthy young virgin, and staring at a tree of primeval forest or blue stars are effective, too.

Furthermore, we had better catch on the spirit or ally that has beautiful glossy blue energy. The spirit or ally is floating like a gas or an image in the inner space, within the earth, or in the universe. If we can see or find it in the daytime or in our dreams at night, you had better catch on it quickly and be given beautiful glossy blue energy by it.

If we succeed in curing or strengthen our livers, we will have the strange power of blue energy like light spring breeze.

I think Mr. Carlos Castaneda might not have died of liver cancer (?) in 1998 if he had practiced some of the above-mentioned ways.

6. Healthy strong heart gives you the feeling of self-confidence and of joy which can cure disease and swallow up an outside object

If we have cured or strengthen our hearts, we can enjoy the same feeling as that of self-confident, joyful, active, sexy, ruthless, good-natured youth or women. Healthy strong heart has the beautiful red energy of such a feeling. Such a red energy can swallow up and burn our dirty energy, the dirty energy of other and devils. So, it can cure our diseases or others' diseases. If it is shot out from our body, it can keep on catching on an outside object, swallow up an object, and burn the bad energy of an object. Light dances wildly in front of our eyes just before such a red energy succeeds in swallowing up our dirty energy, the dirty energy of other, devils, and an outside object. Then, self-pity passes away. So, the feeling of self-confidence, of joy and of ruthless happens to us. Transparent energy and blue energy engulf a star and guard it. Strong beautiful red energy engulfs transparent energy and blue energy, and guards a star from an invader of harmful energy, too.

Regretfully, most of us have thrown away such a red energy after most of us have lost a big love, was divorced, betrayed, beaten, or failed in something, too. As a result, most of us have lost beautiful glossy red color on our complexion or begun to have dirty black red color on our complexion. Stiff shoulder has happened, too. Most of us have become cynical, weak-minded, and stingy. Most of us prefer to gossips about other. Most of us hate taking care of others. At last, horizontal line has begun to be seen between eyes and a strange feeling (a little pain, numbness, impotence) has begun to happen to a little finger. Many red spots have happened to the back of neck. At last, cardiac infarction, angina pectoris, or cancer will happen sooner or later.

★ 3 week fasting makes you excrete a bucketful of old excrement and make your bowel movement regular

To strengthen heart, you had better imagine self-confident, active, sexy, good-natured youth or women, eat bitter foods and massage the thumb's root of your left wrist.

The gates of heart are a small intestine and pancreas. So, you had better strengthen a small intestine and pancreas to strengthen heart, too. To strengthen a small intestine and pancreas, you had better make bowel movement regular. To make bowel movement regular, you had better feel hungry by moving your body well everyday and not eating too much. You had better become a vegetarian as possible. To bowel movement regular, you had better practice fasting for 3 weeks under the supervision of professional when you change job or are fired, too.

★ Beautiful red part of below eyes is an evidence of recovering strong heart

You had better excrete a bucketful of old black excrement in your intestine. You become so relieved and happy that you feel as if you swept a chimney. The first day you excrete your old black excrement, the part just below your eyes will turn to be beautiful red. Acridity, dreariness and self-pity will be removed from your eyes, too. The beautiful red part of your complexion is an evidence of recovering strong heart (in such a case, cancer will never happen to you). Have you such a beautiful red part of your complexion?. Self-confidence and joy will happen to you naturally when beautiful strong red energy of your heart can burns violently again and can be shot out from your body like a flame of a flame-thrower and can swallow up an outside object. You can understand that self-pity will happen to you when red energy of your heart can not do so because your heart is beaten by the stickiness of your dirty energy, of other dirty energy, of devils, and of your complaints (about health, opposite sex, son or daughter, parents, boss, money, work, or post), can't you?

Liver also can be strengthen by excreting a bucketful of old black excrement because liver will not be tortured by the toxin of old black excrement.

★ Why the Scriptures say "fast and pray"?

About for 2 weeks after you finish fasting, you can enjoy happy relieved feeling and can imagine lively. For example, you can imagine Brazil lively. If you have come back to U.S.A from Brazil and can tell someone a lively story about your life in Brazil, your third attention or immaterial fiber can go to Brazil and stay there while telling. The way to confirm the working of your third attention or immaterial fiber is to be able to imagine some place, someone, or some place lively. Then, by the grace of your third attention or immaterial fiber, what you imagine is not an illusion but a reality and the result of realization. So, the Scriptures say "fast and pray". Regrettably, as the pastors of U.S.A become older, they are apt to become fat because of eating too much.

In most cases, such a happy relieved feeling will pass away 2 weeks later after you left a center of fasting. You will begin to eat animal food, animal-protein, much sugar, much salt, drink coffee, alcohol, smoke, do not chew well, do not have a stroll, make ** with opposite sex so that happy relieved feeling will pass away. As the result of happy relieved feeling's passing away, you can neither imagine lively nor change your dream freely, so that your third attention or your immaterial fiber is confined to your energy body or physical body and stops working on for you again. Then, what you imagine or dream is only an illusion or a dream.

About for 2 weeks after you finish fasting, you can imagine lively. It takes some time to be realized. You feel happy just before what you imagine or think of can be realized. There remains some stickiness or the fever of depression in this liveliness.

★ Ironically, selflessness brings a super power of imagination to you

When you can begin to feel so happier that you want to neither accomplish nor gain anything, some stickiness or some fever of depression in this liveliness is eliminated. You become selfless. Then, what you imagine or think of other people or society or psychic world or the universe subtly and lightly without eagerness can be realized only in a few seconds. You feel so weird and fearful when it is realized 10-20 times in succession that you never tell proudly what it is realized. You can not begin to have such a super power of imagination as long as you take advantage of a power of imagination to realize your own wishes.

7. A white stone image of Buddha has given me a burning stone table and a cool black gray stone table. Joyful red energy of heart has to be cooled by cool white foggy energy of lung

About 2 years ago when I put a set of red granite, gray granite, marble, black-tourmaline on the four corners of my bed, I broke through a black red energy area and entered a transparent energy area which was 2-4 km in diameter. I flew upward at an angle from my body and visited there. It was a second visit. There were about 20 black gray stone images of Buddha and a white stone image of Buddha on the left side of stairs. Stone images were about 3 feet in height. When I went up the stairs of stone, a white stone image of Buddha suddenly shot a ray beam weapon toward me. Ray beam pierced through my body like a spear and made my body lifted. Crying "I won't be beaten!", I extinguished the ray beam and came down to the top of a black stone image's head.

A white stone image of Buddha was pleased at my fighting. If I were weak, I should have been exploded to death or were melted to death the moment he shot out at me. He said to me "100 years later, I will eliminate the area where I have lived. Then, I will meet you again. I hope you will keep on tempering and strengthening yourself more until then". He made a woman go to the gate of the area with me and see me off.

★ Why Ancient Egyptian Pyramids have many pieces of gray granites under the layer of marble?

She gave me a present from him at the gate of the area. The present was 2 thin stone tables. Healthy strong kind red fire was burning within one stone table. It was the same fire as that of the woman who saw me off. Her face was black and a little grotesque. Red fire which had the feeling full of affection was burning within her body.

It is a big implication that he presented me two stone tables which are a burning table and a black gray cool stone table. Whenever I put only marbles on the corner of my bed, I feel so hot or vigorous that I begin to feel painful, irritated and can not sleep. Big lust keeps on happening to me. Marble has infrared rays. But, I feel better and comfortable whenever I add a piece of gray cool granite to marbles. He has taught me that only hot red energy or cool energy is harmful to our bodies. Both hot red energy and cool energy are necessary for us.

For example, a powerful engine has to be cooled by air or water. If it were not cooled, it will break down, be fired or exploded to pieces. The more powerful an engine is, the more it has to be cooled. I can have understood why Ancient Egyptian Pyramids have many rectangle gray granites under the layer of marble. Equally, red energy of heart has to be cooled by the cool white fog energy of lung, too. Heart hates excessive hotness. Energetic heart is weakened by excessive hotness, so energetic joyful heart has to be cooled by the sad white energy of lung. To keep on being big men, big men have to have much sadness (kindness, mercy) as well as much joy-ruthless-activity.

8. Some woman's energy body exploded to pieces and was sucked into the white world (heaven, the white spirit's world). So, I gathered up the pieces and hardened them into her former body

When I put this burning stone table on the diseased part of other during my dreaming, I could cure disease. This burning stone table is very strong. When I put it on the diseased womb of some woman during my dreaming at night, her physical body suddenly rolled down from her bed. Furthermore, her energy body exploded to pieces and was sucked into the white spirit's world. This white spirit had descended to me at night several times by then. This white spirit's world was like a fairly vast fog whose size was much bigger than 2-4 km in diameter. I was frightened to think she had died.

I gathered up the pieces of her energy body and hardened them into her former energy body. Then, I boxed her ears and squirted her cold water many times to recover her consciousness. After I recover her consciousness, I brought her energy body to her physical body at different place and put it in her physical body.

★ We can come back to the earth by remembering the ache of flap and the coldness of water on the earth

If we enter into another world or the far distant universe and can remember lively what we have experienced in the ordinary lives on the earth, we can make our energy bodies linked with our first attention that makes up our physical bodies on the earth. As a result, we can come back to the earth. So, to make her remember the ache of flap and the coldness of water on the earth, I boxed her ears and squirted her cold water many times. If we can not remember lively what we have experienced on the earth, we can not come back to the earth. In such a case, we will be killed in another world or the far distant universe, be confined to it or live there for super long years.

9. An owner of a stock farm in Brazil could come back to the earth from Venus by remembering his girlfriend's womb lively

About 2 years ago, my acquaintance who has a stock farm in Brazil could come back to the earth from Venus owing to remembering the womb of his girlfriend's. She said to me "At that time, I felt big ache in my womb". Some day, they and I were siting in some building in Japan. About 5 years ago when I was lying on my back on a bench at the sun-rise in the jungle of Amazon, the transparent ally visited me and winded round my trunk kindly. This transparent ally entered the building in Japan all the way from Brazil and turned round me giving the noise of wind. This ally's length was about 1.5 m. My acquaintance was aware of this ally around me and intuited "It is very strange that a wind begins to blow in the building whose windows have been closed. I will be able to venture out to the universe for the first time if I get on this wind". He was presented the first space travel by this ally and came back to the earth by remembering his girlfriend's womb on the earth. He made a dash at his girlfriend's womb on the earth.

In this respect, you have to have something like a deck of aircraft carrier on the earth if you want to come back to the earth or the ordinary life on the earth safely. Furthermore, if you do not have it, you can not come back from the universe or another world. A deck of aircraft carrier can be compared to your remembering lively one of what your physical body has done on the earth. My acquaintance's deck was his girlfriend's womb.

By the way, my acquaintance has made friends with danger or death. He said to me "In wet season, stock farms are buried by the water (it becomes about 50 m deep during a night) of much rain so that many cows are often drowned. It is dangerous when we can not make our cars run on the muddy road at night because much rain makes road muddy. There are lions outside cars. If we stay in our cars, we may be drowned by the water of much rain". An inorganic ally is apt to like a man of abandon, bravery, decision, and independence. He is such a man as an inorganic ally likes. So, I think an inorganic ally who visited me to Japan all the way from Brazil liked him and took him to Venus for the first time.

★ If we can remember the space travel or another world lively, we can enter there easily. But, we are always confined to the earth owing to always remembering what our physical bodies have done on the earth

If we can forget the touch, sight, hearing, smell, taste of our physical bodies on the earth, we will be able to enter into the universe or another world easily. If we can remember lively what we have experienced in the space travel or another world, we will be able to enter there again easily. We are always confined to the surface of the earth or the ordinary life on the earth owing to always remembering lively what our physical bodies have done on the surface of the earth. Buddha taught so in India 2500 years ago as well as don Juan Matus, the teacher of Carlos Castaneda.

An obsession about something on the surface of earth is both a strong chain to confine us to the earth and a deck of aircraft carrier for us to come back to from the universe or another world. If we want to fly into the universe or another world, we have to throw away illness and complaints. If we have illness, the trouble of spine, or complaints, we are almost always remembering the bad part of our physical bodies and the contents of our complaints in the ordinary lives on the surface of the earth. In such a way, illness and complaints are strong chains and can confine us to the surface of the earth. If we are healthy, we can forget our physical body and lose our complaints in the ordinary lives on the earth. From this additional angle, I often recommend that you had better become healthier if you want to become a psychic astronaut. If we can feel so healthy and happier that we have neither obsession nor wishes on the surface of the earth, we can throw away the strong chains of the earth's surface and fly into the universe or another world. Ally and the spirit can give us peculiar happy feeling, cut our strong chains of the earth's surface and give the ability of the space travel to us, too. That is to say, ally and the spirit give us the peculiar happy feeling which is different from the feeling of what we feel in the ordinary lives on the earth. As a result, they can cut our strong chains of the earth's surface and give the ability of the space travel to us.

10. To break through the dangerous white gate of heaven without being killed, you had better temper yourself

As soon as I put the immaterial burning stone table on the above-mentioned woman's womb during my dreaming, her energy body exploded to pieces. She said "I had felt as if I were on the brink of being sucked into something once a month in my childhood. Then, I had felt fearful, and recited the sutra of Buddhism against it". I told her "You have to enter into the white spirit's world without explosion or fainting. The white spirit's world is one of so-called heavens. You have to temper yourself seriously from now on if you want to enter into one of heavens not being killed. Can you understand the gate of heaven (super long life, the spirit) is narrow? Christ said so. It is very difficult for us to pass through it safely".

She has a husband. So, I could not have told her the same contents as those of what I have written in Part 1-4 (for example, saving sex energy, fasting, concentrating on breath for 3 weeks, stopping breath automatically, body exercise, making friends with danger). If she wants to enter into one of heavens and comes back to the earth freely, she has to practice what I have written in Part 1-4 everyday at least for 10 years so seriously that she wants to become a first-class woman of martial arts. I wonder if she is so serious or crazy as to practice what I have written in Part 1-4. So, I have not told her what I have written in Part 1-4.

Most of us are apt to talk about heavens familiarly without knowing heavens at all. Most of us have neither the loyalty to heavens nor the strength against the strange feeling and super power of heaven. Most of us do not deserve to enter into the heavens. To cure disease, and to gain money, supernatural power and followers, most of us try to take advantage of the power of heavens. But, most of us run away from the heaven and try not to remember it if most of us are permitted to approach the gate of heaven fortunately. Most of us fear.

★ I will have to make an area where I live in the universe or another world, and post securities around the gate

A white stone image of Buddha (who presented 2 pieces of stone tables to me) said to me "100 years later, I will eliminate the area where I have lived", so that I can have understood I will have to make an area where I will live. When I leave the earth forever, I will have to make an area where I live in the universe by using my energy. In most cases, such areas (which I have seen or entered) are made of gassy energy balloons whose size is about 2-4 km in diameter. I will have to make houses, roads, trees, sky, river, animals and so on in such a gassy energy balloon by using my energy, too. I will have to shut out the energies which are like a murderer, robber, thief, fraud, fierce animal, sly snake, parasite, infection, epidemic and plague. I will have to protect my area by weapons. I will have to post securities or a garrison around the gate of my area in the universe.

In most cases when I entered or broke through such a gassy balloon in the universe or the sky, I met a security guard around the gate of it. 2 years ago in the morning I was breaking through another white gassy balloon, a security guard flung off in front of me with a sharp sickle held in his hand. He and I stared at each other for a moment. I said to him"I am on the way to taking a stroll from the earth" and soared into the more upper area. Looking up at me, he talked to himself "I am much surprised that the energy body of a living human being has soared here. At first, I think you are a ghost".

★ We are sandwiched between two kinds of death

We can live on the earth for 100 years at most. We have to be killed by the dirty energy body of other, devils and our complaints (about opposite sex, health, son or daughter, parents, money, boss, work, post and so on) on the earth. They are compared to wolves behind us. Or, we have to be killed by the super power of another world's gate. It can be compared to a tiger in front of us. We are sandwiched between two kinds of death. I think it is manlier for us to try to run a blockade of another world at the risk of our lives than waiting death on the earth.

Another world (heaven, the spirit, and the universe) is made of inorganic energy. If our energy bodies have neither absorb the inorganic energy of another world (or stone, the earth, stars) nor been tempered by the inorganic energy of another world, our weak dirty sticky energy bodies will be exploded or melted to death the moment we approach another world.

★ How to break through such a dangerous narrow gate of another world

To break through such a dangerous narrow gate of another world, strong energy body has to be made of strong healthy physical body(which has strong healthy liver-beautiful blue color energy, strong healthy heart-beautiful red color energy, strong healthy spleen-beautiful yellow color energy, strong healthy lung-beautiful white color energy, strong healthy V-spot on the crest of the sternum at the base of neck-beautiful transparent energy, strong healthy spleen-beautiful yellow energy, and strong healthy kidney-beautiful black color energy) at first.

That is to say, we have to make our strong energy bodies by using strong healthy livers, hearts, lungs, spleens, V-spots, kidneys (by using beautiful blue color energy, red color energy, yellow color energy, white color energy, transparent energy, black color energy of our physical bodies).

To break through the dangerous narrow gate of another world, we have to make our strong healthy energy bodies absorb and get used to the inorganic energy of another world next.

If you can succeed in entering into another world without being killed, you should not be proud of it. You had better dare to enter into more powerful, beautiful, dangerous world tempering your energy body. Needless to say, tempering your energy body and physical body is what I have written in Part 1-7.

11. An offensive ally took me to the tip of some vast flying black universe

I think an ally and the spirit prefer not men or women of timidity, of gloominess, of stinginess, of not-loyalty but men or women of abandon, of largesse, of humor, of loyalty. While you are challenging the dangerous another world at the risk of your life, various allies and spirits surely appear in front of you and help your adventures.

In this respect, pastor. Carlos Annacondia, Morris Cerullo, Rodney Browne, Steve Ryder, Mahesh Chavda are men of abandon, of largesse, and of humor. Furthermore, they have thirsted for the spirits like a baby and kept on having much loyalty to the spirits. They have many features which the spirits love. So, the spirits have come to them and given them the power to cure many diseases, revive the dead, cheer many people and make many people convert to the flock of Christ. They seem to be interested in doing so and do not seem to be interested in becoming a psychic astronaut. But , I think they will be able to venture out to another world (for example, heaven, the spirit's world) or the universe if they want. I think the spirits and allies love them and will help them to do so, too. I feel sorry that a few of them are too fat. A few of them had better lose weight if they want not to lose supernatural power to cure or cheer other people. Furthermore, a few of them had better lose weight if they want to become a psychic astronaut.

★ An offensive ally had guarded me since he was pleased with my fighting

About two and half an years ago, a male ally hid behind my left back disguising as my mother. I asked " Who are you?" because I felt a little strange about him. Don Juan Matus says in the Mr. Carlos Castaneda book "It is the most offensive, dangerous and powerful ally that approaches us disguising as our parents and dear friends". That was right. He suddenly roared "Gou" violently shaking my surroundings. He struck my left shoulder and tried to scoop out my abdomen.

The moment he struck my left shoulder, it was dented 3 inches and came right immediately. If I had been weak, my left shoulder and arm of my energy body would have been lost so that the left side of my physical body would have always felt ache, coldness or numbness and been suffering from illness sooner or later. By the way, the right shoulder and right arm of some young Japanese woman's energy body had been lost until a year ago because she had been attacked by a ally everyday for 6 months. She can make her energy body go anywhere on the earth and come back to her physical body immediately by nature. I think her ability to do so on the earth is equal to that of Ms. Carol Tigges (who is a cohort of the late Mr. Carlos Castaneda). I prevented my abdomen from being scooped out by the offensive, dangerous and powerful ally.

He was pleased with my fighting. He said to me in a haughty tone "I will teach you whatever you want to know. Ask me". For about 6 months since then, he had followed me and guarded me against attacks whenever I entered into new another world of the universe. Although I did not ask him to do so, he drove off any enemy in front of me within a second. He was very kind for me in spite of his haughty tone.

★ Some vast universe was flying in the vaster universe roaring "Gou!"

Some day, I broke through 4 different worlds and reached the tip of some vast universe that had innumerable stars. I felt on the way to it as if I had opened 4 windows in a personal computer in succession. I looked down at the tip of some vast universe with him. Roaring "Gou", the tip of some vast universe was flying in the vaster universe. The vaster universe was dark but emitted faint cool glossy yellow light. On the way to the tip of some vast universe, two enemies attacked me. He drove off them. The moment I was on the brink of being melted to death by a second enemy, he burst away from my rearward and saved me. He has never appeared in front of me since I reached the tip of some vast universe. Since then, I think sometimes I wish I would call for his help. But, I have striven to struggle to survive without his help.

★ By the grace of kind many people, allies and the spirits, I have not become cynical. I owe them much gratitude

I can feel happy sometimes although I had been tortured by my parents, my old bitter trouble and the pang of my spine for long years. Many people, allies and the spirits have helped me. I owe them much gratitude. When I feel depressed, I can begin to feel happy by the grace of remembering their faces. As for me, they look like a so-called God. Fortunately, by the grace of their kindness for me, I have neither become cynical nor withdrawn into myself. I can have tried to be kind for other people as much as possible.

★ It took me 13 years to reach the tip of some flying vast universe

It took me 13 years to reach the tip of some flying vast universe since I began to read Cabala and The Emerald-Tablet of Thoth-The-Atlantean. The first time I read them, I could not understand at all. But, I intuited the contents of them are real. I thought they had been written for me. Since then, I have been interested in becoming another astronaut. I think someone will think so to read my book. Modern astronomy says "The

Regional Galaxy (3 million light-years in radius. Our galaxy belongs to it) is flying to Virgo at the speed of 300 km a second which is 60 million light-years distant from us and has 2000 galaxies. But, Virgo is leaving us toward the south at the speed of 1000 km a second".

12. I was overwhelmed by an unbending, unwavering strong intent of some vast flying black universe's tip that is rushing headlong. I often remember its feeling lively to recover

The tip of some vast universe was dark, but it emitted faint cool glossy yellow light as well as the vaster universe. It had more transparent energy than the vaster universe.

Whenever I flow down or up the transparent energy of my neck's V-spot all over my body, I begin to see my internal organs and to be able to shoot out my energy body (my dreaming body, my immaterial fiber, my third attention) to an outside object. So, I think transparent energy has the function of clearing, and of lubricating. This function gives gloss to other energies (blue, red, white, yellow, and black energies). Other energies can not work on for us smoothly without gloss. Physiognomy says "If a color without gloss appears on the surface of your face, a bad luck will happen to you. Glossy beautiful red, glossy beautiful yellow and glossy beautiful white on the surface of your face are the omens of a good luck".

So, I can have understood that some vast universe can be flying in the vaster universe smoothly with the help of the transparent energy's function. Furthermore, I could felt the unbending, unwavering strong intent of some vast universe's tip. Such intent was to rush headlong. I felt as if innumerable big battleships were flying. I had seen such an unbending, unwavering strong patient intent for the first time. I was overwhelmed by it. Healthy strong kidney brings up strong black energy. Black energy is like black water. Strong black energy can bring up unbending, unwavering strong patient intent. Correctly, I think some vast black universe was not flying but flowing as a big glossy black river in the vaster universe.

As against the unbending, unwavering strong patient intent of some vast black universe's tip, my intent (my immaterial fiber or my third attention) is very weak, wavering and timid. When I am in a weak moment, I remember the feeling of its unbending, unwavering strong intent and am engulfed by such a strong black energy.

★ By the grace of sweet yellow energy, some vast universe can rush headlong more smoothly without much resistance

Excessive transparent black energy without yellow energy is useless. It only keeps on rushing headlong so recklessly and arrogantly as to suicide. There are the same type of people among us because they only have strong healthy kidneys and do not have strong healthy spleens. They rush headlong, fight and ruin. They have only sticks, and do not have carrots.

Strong healthy spleen emits sweet yellow energy. Sweet yellow energy can lay restrain on excessive black energy's activity which healthy strong kidney has. If we rush headlong sweetly, we can rush headlong without much resistance. It can be compared to the famous saying-the carrot and the stick. In addition to transparent glossy energy, the tip of some vast universe had faint beautiful cool dry yellow energy, too. As a result, some vast universe can have kept on rushing headlong more smoothly in the vaster universe.

13. We need both light, glossy, sweet feeling and self-confident, brave feeling of insane genius. If you have not a well-balanced feeling, you will be disgraced by many attacks of others or be looked down upon

In this respect, most of us had in the childhood (1) the feeling of light spring breeze (beautiful blue energy) (2) the feeling of gloss (beautiful transparent energy) (3) the feeling of sweetness (beautiful yellow energy). But, most of us are apt to have thrown away them since adulthood because of the complaints (about opposite sex, health, son or daughter, parents, boss, work, money, or post). Most of us think "I can not believe in others but only in myself " and become cynical. Throwing away them can be compared to a rusty rifle which has not a trench of barrel, a leaf, a sight line.

In such a case, most of us can not fire a bullet (red energy of heart, white energy of lung, black energy of kidney). Most of us can not shoot out useful immaterial fibers or the third attentions to an outside object and can not see, judge or control an outside object well.

Big men, founders, happy-healthy-efficient people are apt not to throw away the feeling of light spring breeze, the feeling of gloss or the feeling of sweetness in spite of complaints.

Their energies, feelings, atmospheres, behaviors, voices and complexion are light, glossy and sweet. They have such good pheromones or attractions to control others without interests or threat. If they have lost such good pheromones or attractions for long time, they will be disgraced by many attacks of others sooner or later.

But, only the feeling of light spring breeze, the feeling of gloss and the feeling of sweetness without (4) the feeling of self-confidence, of abandon, of ruthless, of joy, and of activity (beautiful red energy of heart) (5) or the feeling of insanity and genius (beautiful white energy of lung) (6) or the feeling of rushing headlong and of bravery (beautiful black energy of kidney) are useless. Only the feeling of light spring breeze, the feeling of gloss and the feeling of sweetness can be compared to a rifle without bullets and will be looked down upon sooner or later.

★ You had better hunt various bigger powers and various better feelings as possible

Power is the good feeling. To begin to have better feeling, you had better (1) strengthen your various internal organs, become healthier, and grow at least 10-20 years old younger by what I have written in Part 1-4 (2) be able to stop your breath automatically (3) become on the point of dying or make friends with danger (4) do fasting (5) cure the trouble of spine (6) follow your body-response (7) remember or imagine beautiful strong feeling's scenes (8) eat acid foods to strengthen liver, eat bitter foods to strengthen heart, eat sweet foods to strengthen spleen, eat hot foods to strengthen lung or eat salty foods to strengthen kidney-eat a well-balanced diet (9) be able to shoot out your immaterial fiber or your third attention to an outside object from your body and see it through or control it <If your immaterial fiber or third attention is compelled to be confined to your physical body or your aura, you will feel irritated, self-pity, inferiority complex, guilty, depressed, stuck, indecisive, or fearful > (10) absorb beautiful strong energy from stones , stars, allies and the spirits (11) be presented beautiful strong energy by allies and the spirits (12) enter and see beautiful strong feeling's world in the universe by the grace of allies or the spirits (13) listen to the voices of healthy-happy-efficient people and the voices of founders, big men, pioneers, enterprisers who have not been disgraced and have not been proud or careless (14) listen to the bass drums of the universe (15) listen to the voices which are uttered by the central energy pipe of physical body (16) listen to the silent voice (the voice of God, voice without voice on the back of left ear).

To hunt bigger power as possible, you had better hunt various better feelings as possible by all means. Above-mentioned ways to hunt power and the good feeling are just examples.

Don't be satisfied with one beautiful strong color energy of good feeling. You had better search for more beautiful and stronger same color energies of better feeling as possible. Furthermore, you had better search for beautiful strong different color energies of good feeling as possible.

14. The Scriptures say "The Kingdom (heaven, the spirit) is coming to you. Repent!". The etymology of "Repent!" is to change your bad feeling. Don Juan Matus says "Don't be influenced by the bad feelings of others"

Don Juan Matus says "(Most of) our fellow men are black magicians. Can you deviate from the path that they have lined up for you? If you remain with them, your thoughts and your actions are fixed forever in their terms. That is slavery. The warrior is free from all that"-Tales of Power, "Freedom is expensive, but the price is not impossible to pay. So, fear your captors, your masters. Don't waste your time and your power fearing freedom"-Tales of Power.

"The world of people goes up and down and people go up and down with their world; warriors have no business following the ups and downs of their fellow men"-The Second Ring of Power.

"The recommendation for warriors is not to have any material things on which to focus their power, but to focus it on the spirit, on the true flight into the unknown, not on trivialities"-The Eagle's Gift.

The etymology of "sin" is to miss the target. To miss the target is to concentrate not on good feeling (involving the feeling of ally, of the spirit and of space travel) but on bad feeling. To concentrate on bad feeling is to become powerless. To become powerless is to become unhealthy-unhappy-inefficient or not to become a psychic astronaut. So, change your feeling if you have followed the bad feeling (such as heavy Oil Sea, sludge, mud or sewage) for long time. The Scriptures say "The Kingdom (heaven, the spirit) is coming to you. Repent!". The etymology of "Repent!" is to change your feeling.

# Part 7

---

## Examine

When we have good complexion and good body-response, our assemblage points (the cores of our consciousness) can move into the interior of our bodies and our immaterial fibers (or the third attention) can shoots out from our bodies. Then, we can accomplish something. In such a case, we are neither proud nor careless. We are not in illusion but in reality. That is to say, we can say that we have dependable good self-importance, self-image and trust. To accomplish something, we had better examine whether or not we have dependable good self-importance, self-image and trust.

1. Eating in moderation is indispensable to become happy-healthy-efficient

2. Eating too much makes my immaterial fiber confined to my body so that I become a blockhead

3. The key point of master's physiognomy is eating in moderation and good complexion

4. My acquaintance could not become a Prime Minister of Japan because eating too much. Kennedy Junior was an epicure or had bad complexion?

5. Sink in the hell willingly and you can break through the bottom of the hell. Welcome an insult to you sometimes a month

6.Some leading disciple of Buddha had never complained about his poor living and meditated earnestly

7.The priest of Jaina religion in India lives with his body daubed by mud

8. A petty tyrant

9. While throwing away your self-importance temporarily and groveling before a petty tyrant, you make a strategy to win and wait for a good timing patiently

10. Challenge to multiply happy lucky feeling under a difficult condition

11.Writing about a petty tyrant touches me on a sore place

12. We need only good self-importance accompanying comfortable body-response which can realize what we imagine. We can have good self-importance only when we have good complexion. Buddha taught us how to trust and what to trust

13.The Eagle is a mass of black energy shot out by the earth

14. I saw the innumerable cores of human being's dead energy bodies which were the Eagle's food 20 years ago

15. It seems to be difficult for only Tensegrity to make the fire burn from within your body and clean up the central energy pipe of your body

16. Denting navel and constricting anus 100 times everyday is the most effective to make the fire burn from within

17. Repentance may be the most effective if you have been as very devious and stubborn as don Juan Matus had been for long years

18. Nagual Julian Osario threw don Juan Matus who could not swim into the flood. He always walked along the edge of abyss. I had been nearly killed by injection in my childhood in China

19. The right way of walking is a good weapon to fight against Old Age. Then, the sky just above the horizon is the secret door of another world

20. Reading many books can weaken your body and heart. Be careful not to be influenced by the bad feeling (?) of Mr. Carlos Castaneda

21. You had better imagine Christ and Paul who did not fear the death and devoted themselves to the spirit, and can move your assemblage point deeply. Imagine Napoleon, too

22. You had better enter into another world through voice or sound. Absorb the feelings of various flights

23 Don't underestimate the death defier because she has special strong calm energy which can move within the universe freely

24. My next subject is to research the secret of gravity that is black energy

25. Regrettably, the more we can recognize our stupidity deeply, the more we can become healthier and more efficient

26.Say thank you to Mr. Carlos Castaneda, publishing companies, earnest readers, allies, the spirits, many kind people and my wife

NEXT Text

1. Eating in moderation is indispensable to become happy-healthy-efficient

To become happy-healthy-efficient or a psychic astronaut, you had better often examine whether or not (1) you eat in moderation (2) have good complexion (3) sometimes welcome a insult to you or fall into the hell voluntarily or occupy your time with something else (anything would do)(4) make friends with danger or death (5) enjoy taking advantaging of a petty tyrant to temper yourself (6) have good self-importance (7) have dependable trust (8) have good repentance (9) burn the fire from within your body and clean up the central energy pipe of your body(10) walk in the right way (11) say thank you. I intend to explain them by turns.

According to The Second Ring of Power by the late Mr. Carlos Castaneda, a warrior eats four mouthfuls of food quietly and slowly at one time, a while later eats in such a way. Furthermore, a warrior walks miles and miles everyday, too. I think we can not become neither happy-healthy-efficient nor a psychic astronaut unless we eat in moderation. Yoga book says "However we endeavor, we can not succeed in accomplishing the purpose of yoga unless we eat in moderation". The purpose of yoga is to be able to shoot out our immaterial fibers (which is called Samyama in yoga world) or third attention (which is called Purusha in yoga world) to an object from our bodies, judge it, and control it. The last purpose of yoga is to be able to recognize our third attention like a smoke in a treasure-chest, handle it, and catch on the spirits.

2. Eating too much makes my immaterial fiber confined to my body so that I become a blockhead

Ancient Buddhist priests ate once a day by noon. When I visited most their remains in India about 20 years ago, I thought they walked for 5-6 hours everyday to gather foods around other ordinary people's houses. After enough walks, they sat and meditated everyday. Owing to enough walks, long sitting and meditation could not weaken their bodies or hearts. To the contrary, most of us are apt to go anywhere by car and eat too much. Furthermore, most pastors and psychic teachers are apt to pray, read doctrines, sing, meditate and worry about management (money?) everyday without a walk or body exercise. So, our and their physical bodies are apt to weaken by the lack of a walk and of body exercise and by eating too much.

I am apt to eat too much and quickly. I have tried to finish eating before sunset, but failed in doing so. I weigh 10 kilograms over the standard weight. Whenever I eat dinner too much after sunset, I can neither shoot out my immaterial fiber or third attention to an outside object from my body nor change my dream easily. In such a case, I can not concentrate my immaterial fiber or third attention on anything at all. The ability to stop breath automatically, the ability to imagine happy good feeling, the ability of supernatural power and the ability to enter into the universe or another world declines, too. I am confined to stickiness, the fever of depression, coldness, or numbness like heavy Oil Sea, sludge, and sewage. I feel as if the gate of another world or of the universe closed. I am confined to irritation, self-pity, foolishness, indecision and timidity that are the core of unhappy-unhealthy-inefficient individual and home. Next day, it is fairly difficult for me to shoot out my immaterial fiber or third attention from my body. I am still fairly like a blockhead.

I am so foolish that I have failed in eating in moderation and failed in losing my weight since 10 years ago. Although I have understood the obstacle of eating too much and of fatness, I have failed. So, since 3 years ago I have decided not to order new business suit before I succeed in losing my weight by 10 kilograms. Now, there have remained 1-2 proper business suites. I have been in deadly earnest to try to lose my weight since 20 days ago.

I have tried to eat four mouthfuls of food at one time in the morning. I have tried to chew a mouthful of food 100 times. I have tried to eat so at one time in the afternoon. I have eaten so twice a day since 20 days ago so that I have lost my weight by 5 kilograms. I will have to lose my weight by more 5 kilograms.

I have practiced 3 week-fasting 5 times since 20 years ago. When I finished 3 week-fasting, I lost my weight by 8-10 kilograms. I excreted a bucketful of old black excrement (4-5 kilograms), so I lost my weight precisely by

4-5 kilograms. After fasting, every food becomes delicious. I have good appetite so that I am apt to eat too much and gain weight again.

When I concentrate on my breath almost all day during fasting, I can feel that stickiness, the fever of depression, coldness and numbness in my body begin to resolve and exhaust from my shoulder like a dirty gray smoke. I can feel that fasting can discharge bad unnecessary energy from my body and purify my body. It is such a bad unnecessary energy that makes our immaterial fibers or third attention shut into our bodies like a bird in heavy Oil Sea and makes us like a blockhead. Devils and dirty energies of others like such a bad unnecessary energy of ours that they stick to it like vultures, hyenas or maggots. When I cure a patient or teach someone, I feel I am often attacked by the devil which has stuck to a patient or someone.

3.The key point of master's physiognomy is eating in moderation and good complexion

Mr. Nanboku Mizuno (1756-1834), the most famous Japanese man of physiognomy said "Good luck is dependent on eating in moderation. However good physiognomy (look) you have, misfortune will happen to you sooner or later as long as you eat too much or are an epicure. However bad physiognomy you have, considerable or moderate luck will happen to you as long as you eat in moderation or are not an epicure".

He was out of a gangster. To study physiognomy, he worked for a barber, public bath and crematory. He studies as far as many sex organs and anus.

The more he studied physiognomy, the more mistakes he made in physiognomy. Some day, he guessed that eating in moderation and not-being an epicure are the most important points of physiognomy. Since then, he asked "Are you apt to eat too much or are you a epicure?" before he predicted someone's luck. As a result, he could hit the mark ten times out of ten about predicting many people's future lucks. So, he could become so famous for physiognomy that he had more than 1000 disciples in Japan about 200 years ago.

In addition, he thought that the second most important point of physiognomy next to eating in moderation is beautiful glossy color of red, of yellow, and of white on the surface of face. He said "Pale blue, pale white, dirty black red, dirty yellow, not-glossy red, not-glossy yellow, not-glossy white and not-glossy black on the surface of face are the omens of misfortune. Beautiful glossy color of red, of yellow, and of white on the surface of face is the omen of good luck". If your internal organ weakens, dirty not-glossy color will happen to the part of your face's surface where there is the gate or entrance of energy channel connected with your internal organ.

When good complexion happens to you, good bowel movement, good sleeping, soft shoulder, good sex, subtle breath, rejuvenation(grow at least 10-20 years younger) happen to you, too. As a result, you do not feel stuck, can get rid of poor, flabby, fat, or stiff abdomen-waist-hip-thigh, and enjoy happy good feeling. In such a case, the color of your dream is not dirty dark color but a beautiful lively color.

You are suffering from misfortune as long as the color of your dream is dirty dark, pale, dirty black red, dirty brown, not-glossy, or not-lively. When you can enjoy a beautiful glossy lively dream, good luck happens to you. When you begin to eat in moderation or practice fasting, you will be able to begin to dream a beautiful glossy lively dream.

Mr. Nanboku Mizuno, the famous man of physiognomy said "The origin of poverty, downfall, disease, discord (over wife, husband, son, daughter, junior partner, associate, fellow worker or boss), sterility, divorce, juvenile delinquent, accident or dying young is eating too much or being a epicure. The misfortune's origin of son or of daughter is parent's eating too much or parent's being a epicure. Those who are suffering from such a misfortune had better eat in moderation or stop being a epicure and can emerge from such a misfortune. That is the most important secret of my physiognomy".

4.My acquaintance could not become a Prime Minister of Japan because of eating too much. Kennedy Junior was a epicure or had bad complexion?

My acquaintance could not become a Prime Minister of Japan and died of cancer several years ago. Owing to his attributive that was the same as that of a warrior such as abandon, largess, humor, ruthlessness, cunning, patience, sweetness and making friends with danger or death, he started from scratch and rose to No 2 in the Japan political world. He had keen scent, ran the risk of losing whatever he possessed after careful calculation and could shoot out his immaterial fiber or third attention to an object from his body. I can remember that he often emitted his third attention from his body about 25 years ago. He had often burned from within his abdomen. I had liked him because he had much same attributive as that of a warrior which was explained by don Juan Matus. He had taught me about it involuntarily for about 25 years. I owe him much gratitude.

Some day, he asked me in secret "Do you think I will be able to become a Prime Minister?". I replied to him "If you keep on being healthy, you will surely become a Prime Minister sooner or later. But, I think it matters little if you can become a Prime Minister or not. You had better do any good act for Japan or the world that is thought of by you as if you were a Prime Minister. Now that you have become one of the bosses and have big influence over the Japan political world, you can do so from now on. As long as you do so, you never become mortified if you can not become a Prime Minister. Without the post of a Prime Minister, you can do the same work as that of a Prime Minister if you want". He was much pleased to hear my thought. He said to me " Good advice. You can really have began to talked good thing, can't you?".

After all, the big man of the Japan political world died of cancer not becoming a Prime Minister of Japan. I think it was because that he ate too much, was fat and began to have bad complexion little by little. His wife said to me"I have often said to my husband that '"For your health, you had better live in moderation'". But, he never follows my advice. I have given up".

Kennedy Junior (the son of the former U.S.A president) died in his own airplane crash over the Pacific in the summer of 1999. I wonder if he had eaten too much or been an epicure? Furthermore, I wonder if he had bad complexion?

In this respect, you can judge soundly what you do with the help of your complexion. Whatever you do is proper as long as your complexion becomes better so that you can grow younger.

There are hundreds of ways to temper yourself, to live or to enjoy. They are like a maze, too. You must look at every way closely and deliberately. You had better follow it as long as it can give good complexion, rejuvenation, comfortable body-response and happy lucky feeling to you.

5. Sink in the hell willingly and you can break through the bottom of the hell. Welcome a insult to you sometimes a month

According to the Buddhist precepts, followers had better (1) eat once by noon, not eat animal food or animal-protein (2) not drink alcohol, not smoke (3) not make love with opposite sex (4) not kill (5) not thieve (6) not tell a lie (7) not make up (8) sleep on the mat on the earth (not sleep or sit on gorgeous bed or chair)-on 8th, 14th, 15th, 23rd, 29th and 30th day every month as possible.

In a broad sense, (7)(8) means being well content with our present lives, being modest, compromise, not glossing ourselves or not being competitive. For example, I sometimes behave as the foot of some meeting, of some party, or of some group when I attend it. I behave as if I were a blockhead or ill, too. I welcome a insult to me or a contempt for me. I am pleased to be beaten on such a day. I sometimes follow these precepts as possible. Then, I feel better and relieved. You had better try only for a day. You will surely feel so, too. You will think reading my book pays you well.

Such a way is the fifth principle of the stalking's arts which is "When faced with odds that can not be dealt with, warrior retreat for a moment. They let their minds meander. They occupy their time with something else. Anything would do" (The Eagle's Gift). That is to say, we don't have to bear a heavy load of competition, of ranking, of love, of trouble, of disease, of complaint, of grudge, of fear, of irritation, of self-pity, of guilt and of much sadness everyday. Sometimes, we had better throw away such a heavy load. How to throw away it is not to run away from it but to welcome it.

When we fall into deep water, we will die if we flounder desperately to save under water. If we sink in deep water obediently, we will come to the surface automatically. Sometimes, we had better welcome so-called hell and sink in it as deeply as possible. Then, ironically, we can break through the bottom of the hell or the hell will run away from us. Such a way is to make friends with danger or death, too. A hero, general, founder, pioneer and enterpriser are good at such a way. The most famous Japanese general of old age, Kenshin Uesugi said "If we strive to save, we will be killed. If we strive to die, we will be saved".

We can sometimes cure a terminal cancer or a depression if we don't follow the advice of doctor. My another acquaintance ran works and cured a terminal cancer of spinal cord. His doctor said that he would die in a month. He said to me about 3 years ago " I decided not to die on the bed of hospital but to die working in my works. I threw away medicine". He left the hospital and began to work in his works. He could walk only 50 m at first. He could cure the incurable cancer of spinal cord but some small holes had remained on his spinal cord and his spinal cord had become bent.

6. Some leading disciple of Buddha had never complained about his poor living and meditated earnestly

Some leading disciple of Buddha never complained about whatever foods he was given by ordinary other people or however rudely he was given foods by ordinary other people 2500 years ago in India. He approached ordinary other people calmly and modestly as if he had been clear Moon. He never complained about whatever clothes he wore, too. He enjoyed wearing clothes that were made of thrown-away rag. When a Hunsen's patient gave him food, a rotten finger of a Hunsen's patient dropped into his bowl together with food, he ate both the food and the rotten finger in his bowl calmly.

Buddha told him "You do not have to walk around other ordinary people's houses to gather foods because you become old. You had better sit beside me and eat foods with me everyday which my followers bring to me. You had better wear neat clothes which my followers bring to me, too". Buddha asked him why he did so. Then, he replied "Someone will be able to become selfless and calm down at night if someone of future generation knows that such a leading disciple of Buddha as me kept on gathering and eating poor meals, wearing poor clothes, and meditating in the wood seriously everyday in spite of old age. In this respect, I have kept on doing an act of charity for many people of future generation. I have been giving good feeling power to many people of future generation". Buddha was very pleased to hear his answer.

7. The priest of Jaina religion in India lives with his body daubed by mud

The priests of Jaina (spelling?) religion in India daub mud on all over their bodies and live in such a way. Jaina religion was founded 2500 years ago in India. It has 400-500 thousand rich followers like merchants of jewelry. I saw they were daubing mud on all over their bodies in front of some stream when I visited India 20 years ago. At first, I thought they were washing with mud of some stream. But, I mistook the meaning of such a way because they were walking in a town with their bodies daubed by mud. To practice becoming selfless, abandoning themselves and calming down (being patient) under difficult conditions, they seem to be living in such a way. Such a way seems like writing "STUPID" with paint on forehead and walking calmly in a town.

Most of us or all of us will be driven to the last ditch or humiliate ourselves at least once or twice in the course of life. If we always get upset, break down into tears, or go out of the way in such a case, we will ruin. While we are letting it take the course of nature for a while and calm down under difficult conditions, body-response will happen to you. Then, you will tempt the fate following your body-response to your surroundings. I often wish I could live writing "STUPID" with paint on my forehead in Japan. Some day, I will visit India again and walk with my body daubed by mud.

Such a way is the same as that of our energy body's space travel. Buddha said "Our energy bodies will fall into the hell if our energy bodies fall into the interior of the earth headfirst". We will crash through the other side of the earth and sink in the universe at super high speed if we dare to fall into the interior of the earth headfirst. Furthermore, we can ascend in the universe automatically at super high speed if we sink in the universe headfirst without fear nor panic. It is one of the ways for our energy bodies to venture out of our physical bodies to the far distant universe. Somehow, I have an attachment to the galaxy called Big Magellan Cloud which is 160 thousand light-years distant from the earth and just below the earth.

Furthermore, such a way is control which is one of stalking's six elements (control, discipline, forbearance, timing, will, and the petty tyrant).

8. A petty tyrant

Don Juan Matus said in the book with the title-The Fire From Within"A petty tyrant is a tormentor. Someone who either holds the power of life and death over warriors or simply annoys them to distraction". According to The Fire From Within, there are 4 kinds of tyrants. It says "The tyrant (the Eagles, the black spirit, the black energy of the universe) is the one and only ruler in the universe", " A petty tyrant is the most fearsome, tyrannical man who is a buffoon(involving other color energies of the universe, the other color spirits and ally).A little petty tyrant persecutes and inflicts misery but without actually causing anybody's death. A small-fry petty tyrant is only exasperating and bothersome to no end".

I think that complaint (about opposite sex-divorce-big lost love-dis-
cord, son or daughter, health, parents, money, work or post), devils, dirty
energy body of other, our dirty energy (stickiness, the fever of depression,
coldness, numbness), the disordered part of spine, eating too much, and
bad complexion are petty tyrants (buffoons) or little petty tyrant or
small-fry petty tyrant, too. Furthermore, I think unhappy-unhealthy-
inefficient people and founders, big men, pioneers, enterprisers who will
become disgraced in 3-5 years seem to become a little petty tyrant or
small-fry petty tyrant because they are apt to persecute or anger or bother
other people to no end. They are not grateful but a grumbler. They are
proud or careless. They take so many liberties.

A petty tyrant, a little petty tyrant, a small-fry petty tyrant have bad
complexion, bad bowel movement, bad appetite, bad sleeping, bad sex,
stiff shoulder, poor or flabby abdomen and rough breath. They seem as if
they made every effort to transmit their pains to other people. They seem
as if they were epidemic germs.

"To be defeated by a small-fry petty tyrant is not deadly, but devastat-
ing. The degree of mortality, in a figurative sense, is almost as high. By
that I mean that warriors who succumb to a small-fry petty tyrant are
obliterated by their own sense of failure and unworthiness". " To act in
anger, without control and discipline, to have no forbearance, is to be
defeated (by the petty tyrant). ""What happens after warriors are
defeated?"" They either regroup themselves or abandon the quest for
knowledge (the third attention, silent knowledge, the spirit, moving their
assemblage points to the point of undoubt, shooting out the third attention from body, stopping breath automatically, arriving or looking at two
different places at the same moment, voice without voice, the universe)
and join the ranks of the petty tyrant for life"(The Fire From Within).

9. While throwing away your self-importance temporarily and groveling before a petty tyrant, you make a strategy to win and wait for a good
timing patiently

According to the book-The Fire from Within, you had better welcome
a petty tyrant when you meet a petty tyrant. To temper yourself and
enjoy yourself, you had better take advantage of a petty tyrant. While
throwing away your self-importance temporarily, being pleased to be
given a whipping by a petty tyrant and fulfilling a petty tyrant's most

foolish demands, you had better watch a petty tyrant's weakness and make a well-thought strategy and wait for a good timing to win a petty tyrant patiently. According to the book-The Fire From Within, such a control, discipline, forbearance, timing are the attributes of warriorship.

Instead of indulging in self-pity or the wear and tear or hate, you had better begin to have such a brass nerve as you try to temper yourself playing with a petty tyrant. Don't deal with a petty tyrant seriously. Play with a petty tyrant.

Furthermore, fighting against a petty tyrant can give you the ability to meet and deal with the tyrant (Eagle, black energy, the strong black spirit) safely. Such a ability is bravery, patience, self-possession, humor, decision, loyalty and independence.

Happy lucky feeling is power. Don Juan Matus said in the book that the sum of happy lucky feeling can decide your destiny and how to live. You can shoot out your immaterial fiber or third attention to a petty tyrant only when you have happy lucky feeling. When you are given a whipping by a petty tyrant, you had better not lose the same happy lucky feeling as those of light spring breeze, abandon, largess, ruthless, clarity, sweetness, inner silence, kindness, humor, patience, rushing headlong as possible. Under a difficult condition, you had better have the happy lucky feeling of your eyes, of your speaking and of your behavior. In such a case, you can keep on burning the fire within your abdomen and can shoot out your immaterial fiber or third attention to a petty tyrant at a good timing to win a petty tyrant. If we are temporarily pleased to be given a whipping by a petty tyrant, we can end up neither making the fire within your body go out nor throwing away such a happy lucky feeling.

10. Challenge to multiply happy lucky feeling under a difficult condition

But, when most of us meet a petty tyrant, most of us make the fire within abdomens go out, throw away such a happy lucky feeling and indulge in self-pity, irritation, hate or undependable positive self-image. In such a case, bad complexion, bad bowel movement, bad appetite, bad sleeping, looking older, stiff shoulder, poor or flabby abdomen and rough breath happen to most of us. Most of us begin to have the unhappy unlucky feeling of eyes, of speaking and of behavior. In such a case, our immaterial fibers or third attention are confined to our bodies. We can not shoot out our immaterial fibers or third attention to a petty tyrant from our bodies so that we can neither judge a petty tyrant accurately nor win a petty tyrant.

If you are defeated by a petty tyrant, you will indulge in much more self-pity, irritation and hate. You will become cynical and withdraw into yourself. Or, you will become a new petty tyrant or a new small-fry petty tyrant. Then, worse complexion, worse bowel movement, worse appetite, worse sleeping, worse sex, looking much older, stiffer shoulder, and rougher breath happen to you. As a result, we will not be able to shoot out our immaterial fiber or third attention so that we will become unhappy-unhealthy-inefficient like a toothless tiger. Then, we will be suffering from cancer, heart disease or paralysis sooner or later. A petty tyrant will accomplish his purpose to defeat you completely at last.

If you want to become a happy-healthy-efficient man, a warrior, a man of knowledge or a psychic astronaut, you have to multiply the happy lucky feeling or mood (power) about your thought, eyes, voice, behavior in spite of your living in the difficult ordinary world for the purpose of being able to shoot out your immaterial fiber or third attention to an object. If you throw away such a happy lucky feeling and can not multiply such a happy lucky feeling under a difficult condition, such a happy lucky feeling is not yours but a borrowed thing.

I have written in my book-How to concentrate on your breath and stop it automatically (in Japanese) " Those who can multiply happy lucky feeling under a difficult condition have a qualification of powerful man, of wise man, of a patient man. It is a statesman that can make many other people involving himself multiply their happy lucky feeling under a difficult condition. Such a man has flexible and firm abdomen, and has the beautiful fire and power within his abdomen. In addition, following body-response, a powerful man, wise man or patient man can erase his unhappy feeling, multiply his happy lucky feeling or recover from disease under a difficult condition. Such a man can be called a efficient manager, too" 7 years ago. It is such a man that is described for a sheepherder in the Scriptures. By the way, are you a powerful man, wise man, patient man, statesman, efficient manager or good sheepherder for you, your family, your friends or society?

According to The Power of Silence, don Juan Matus said " When we feel worthless, we should be fighting, not apologizing or feeling sorry for ourselves, and that it does not matter what our specific fate is as long as we face it with ultimate abandon".

"The new seers used petty tyrants not only to get rid of their self-importance, but to accomplish the very sophisticated maneuver of moving themselves out of this world" (The Fire From Within).

"Only as a warrior can one withstand the path of knowledge (silent knowledge, the third attention, the spirit, moving the assemblage point to the point of undoubt, voice without voice, seeing, arriving or looking at two different places at the same moment, stopping breath automatically). A warrior can not complain or regret anything. His life is an endless challenge, and challenges can not possibly be good or bad. Challenges are simply challenges" (The Tales of Power).

"Warriors have an ulterior purpose for their acts, which has nothing to do with personal gain. The average man acts only if there is the chance for profit. Warriors act not for profit, but for the spirit" (The Power of Silence).

"The basic difference between an ordinary man and a warrior is that a warrior takes everything as a challenge, while an ordinary man takes everything as a blessing or as a curse" (The Tales of Power).

11. Writing about a petty tyrant touches me on a sore place

While I am writing about a petty tyrant, the parable of a petty tyrant touches me on a sore place. As for me, the complaint about my parents, the old bitter trouble, the pangs of spine, the stiff lamp of my underbelly, and my frequent urination had been a petty tyrant for about 20 years. Such a petty tyrant had made me irritated. Such a petty tyrant had made me have a terrible temper. I had sometimes lost my temper with my 3 daughters, a son, and my wife, and outrage them. I had been neither a good father nor a good husband. I had nearly become a new petty tyrant for them. I had been nearly defeated by my petty tyrant, but I had barely overcome it 2 years ago.

My petty tyrant had nearly deprived me of happy lucky feeling(power) such as peace, sweetness, cunning, joy, clarity, inner silence and flexibility. My eyes , my voice and my behavior had nearly lost happy lucky feeling for long years. My petty tyrant had made my immaterial fiber or third attention almost dead or useless so that my petty tyrant had made me become almost a blockhead for about 20 years.

If I had been weak or impatient, I had been died of bladder cancer or high blood pressure. My petty tyrant had kept on torturing, weakening and trying to kill me for about 20 years, but it had fairly given me the attributive of a warrior which is control, discipline, forbearance, timing while I was barely fighting against my petty tyrant. Such a petty tyrant had been both an enemy and a benefactor for me.

Don Juan Matus was a yaqui Indian and had been much persecuted by Conquest. I think don Juan Matus is stronger than me and the late Mr. Carlos Casteneda, because don Juan Matus had been confronted with much bigger petty tyrants than we had been confronted with, and had overcome them. Don Juan Matus had tempered himself owing to much bigger tyrants. The late Mr. Carlos Castaneda had accomplished a great achievement to write good books. But, I think the late Mr. Carlos Castaneda could not become a successor to don Juan Matus because he seemed to neither been confronted with a much bigger tyrant nor overcome it.

12. We need only good self-importance accompanying comfortable body-response which can realize what we imagine. We can have good self-importance only when we have good complexion. Buddha taught us how to trust and what to trust, too

There are two kinds of self-importance. A good self-importance is to imagine happy good feeling, positive thinking, or positive self-image and make it realize because we can shoot out our immaterial fibers or our third attention from our bodies to an object, judge and control it. Just before it is realized, such a comfortable body-response as that of what I have written in Part 5-Body-Response will happen to us. Such a comfortable body-response is as followers-(1) a tickle happens at the top of head and descends to the back, waist, and womb (in such a case, assemblage point moves into the interior of the body and can feel accurate decision making or judgment without an illusion) (2) see the Nagual (the subtle third attention or the spirit) (3) see the immaterial fiber of the universe (4) sound happens in the recess of throat as if a wooden pipe were snapped (5) feel as if a cave opened in the abdomen and energy ascends from the abdomen (6) overwhelming premonition (7) can hear the voice without uttering on the back of ear (8) feel as if we could perceive about two places or exist at two places simultaneously (9) begin to feel relieved and relaxed(10) begin to take a deep breath(11) stiff abdomen turns to be fluid and relaxed(12) feel beautiful (13) feel a click.

Only when good complexion, good sleeping, good appetite, good bowel movement, good sex, soft shoulder, rejuvenation, subtle breath happen to us, such a body-response happen to us and we can shoot out our immaterial fibers or third attention from our bodies so that we can have a good self-importance. In such a case, our assemblage points-the cores of our consciousness move to the point of undoubt so that we can trust our happy good feelings, positive thinking, or positive self-image.

★ A rotten self-importance is self-pity when our immaterial fiber can not be shot out

To the contrary, a rotten self-importance is to imagine happy good feeling, positive thinking, or positive self-image and not to be able to make it realize because we can not shoot out our immaterial fibers or our third attention from our bodies to an object.

Such a case, comfortable body-response will never happen to us while imaging. Bad complexion, bad sleeping, bad appetite, bad bowel movement, bad sex, stiff shoulder, growing older and rough breath make our immaterial fiber or third attention confined to our bodies so that we have a rotten self-importance. Then, our assemblage points can not move into the interior of our bodies. If we trust false happy good feelings, false positive thinking, or positive self-image, we will be proud, conceited, arrogant, or blowers. Big men, founders, pioneers or enterprisers always have rotten self-importance before they are disgraced. Then, they become proud, conceited, arrogant, or blowers ignoring body-response or not-waiting body-response.

If we keep on having rotten self-importance and fail in realizing happy good feeling, positive thinking, or positive self-image in succession, we will begin to keep on indulging in self-pity.

Buddha said in India 2500 years ago "We had better examine whether or not we can trust what we imagine, think, or plan. We have to learn how to trust or what to trust as possible". Don Juan Matus says "What we need to do to allow magic to get hold of us is to banish doubts from our minds. Once doubts are banished, anything is possible" (Power of Silence).

13. The Eagle is a mass of black energy shot out by the earth

I sometimes see the earth shoots out several big black streams to the universe. I sometimes see the sun shoots out about 4 big black streams to the universe, too. Furthermore, a big black stream of the sky arches from the south to the north. I think Eagle is a stream which a mass of black energy shoots out. Gravity seems like a mass of black energy. When I looked at the lower part of the Eagle which is shot out by a mass of black energy of the earth, it seems to stand erect as an eagle stands, its height reaching to infinity. But, it twists through the sky. Its height seems to be 2-3 times higher than that of earth's diameter.

I saw the lower part of Eagle which stands erect on Turkmen and Uzbek a few times 2 years ago. I saw many female angels floating in this Eagle. The diameter of this Eagle was about the same as that of Caspian Sea. When I concentrate my attention on Eagle in the daytime, I feel the sky and the inner space suddenly become dark. At the time, someone beside me seems to feel so.

I think one way to venture out to the far distant universe is to enter into the Eagle of the earth and rush headlong in it, and venture out to the far distant universe from the tip of the earth's Eagle.

14. I saw the innumerable cores of human being's dead energy bodies which were the Eagle's food 20 years ago

When I was at the second floor of my house in the daytime about 20 years ago, it suddenly grew darker. I was engulfed by beautiful glossy jet-black energy. The death was standing in front of me as a tree of light whose height was about 3 feet. Then, I peeped at Tokyo and glanced at innumerable jet-black thin flat hides like wet fallen leaves. They were the cores of the dead human being's energy bodies. They were floating within the layer 3 feet thick over the surface of Tokyo. As soon as I glanced at them, they suddenly approached me all the way from Tokyo immediately (It takes about 45 minutes to reach my city from Tokyo by train) like gust and engulfed me. They were fishy and a little sticky. They resembled rotten wet fallen leaves. One of them approached the death in my room and ascended along the death silently like a firefly.

Since then, I have hated rotten fallen leaves because they make me remember the cores of the dead energy bodies that had become the Eagle's food at last. Furthermore, I have begun to hate a energy body of a living human being which approaches me or sticks to me however beautiful or

strong or healthy it is. It is because it has fishy smell and the same atmosphere as that of the dead energy body's core much or less.

In this respect, I think all contents of Mr.Carlos Castaneda's books are
not illusional but real. Such an experience had been mysterious since 20
years ago. When I began to read The Eagle's Gift by Mr. Carlos Castaneda
since 7 years ago, I could have understood for the first time that I saw the
Eagle's food (black spirit's food) and the death.

15. It seems to be difficult for only Tensegrity to make the fire burn
from within your body and clean up the central energy pipe of your body

I think we can practice Tensegrity more merrily than other body exercise.
Tensegrity can balance our energy and make our awareness keen. But, I
think it is fairly difficult for us to make the fire burn from within and to
clean up our central energy pipes of our bodies with the help of Tensegrity.

The homepage of infoseek (abcnews.go.com) says that The Associated
Press LOSANGELS reported on June in 1998 Mr. Carlos Castaneda died
of liver cancer on April 27 in 1998. He was believed to be 72. The Los
Angeles Times reported that he was cremated immediately and his ashes
were spirited away to Mexico. The relationship with his daughter, opposite sexes and his parents or the guilt about his childhood friend who was
injured by him seemed to have deprived Mr. Carlos Castaneda of light
spring breeze's feeling and joy. If we lose such a happy good feeling, liver
and heart will weaken. As a result, we will have bad complexion and have
to die of cancer, heart disease or high blood pressure sooner or later at last.

If we can make the fire burn from within and clean up our central
energy pipes, we can recover the good feeling of light spring breeze, of joy
and of bravery and can strengthen liver, heart and kidney. As a result, good
complexion, rejuvenation, good bowel movement, good sleeping, good
appetite, good sex and subtle breath can happen to us. Furthermore, we
can easily thank someone, some beautiful scene, some food, the earth and
so on so that we can recover from such a disease. It is the energy of our
central energy pipes that is so-called inner-God or Phenix or the strongest
third attention.

16. Denting navel and constricting anus 100 times everyday is the most
effective to make the fire burn from within

I think (1) doing bowel movement 6 times, denting navel 100 times in succession, constricting anus 100 times in succession everyday (2) 3 week-fasting (3) concentrating on your breath almost all day for 3 weeks (4) tempering your energy by the way of Chinese style (5) beckoning the spirits (6) following your body-response are the most effective to make the fire burn from within and to clean up your central energy pipe of your body.

Next to the most effective ways are as follows. (7) repenting yourself (8) making your head pay attention to the universe, your abdomen pay attention to the inner space, and your feet pay attention to the interior of the earth simultaneously as often as possible whenever you are free (9) concentrating on your attention on your central energy pipe and clean up it everyday (10) drinking 1.8 liter warm water with a little salt just before sun-rise everyday for 2 weeks once a year and vomit it from the stomach (don't do so if you are suffering from high blood pressure, heart disease, or heavy stomach ulcer).

(11) The right way of walking-"The warrior, first by curling his finger, draws attention to the arms; and then by looking, without focusing your eye, at any point directly in front of you on the arc that starts at the tip of your feet and ends above the horizon, you literally flood your tonal (the right side of your body, the first attention) with information. The tonal became silent" (Tale of Power) (12) the not-doing of looking at something, looking at something with eyebrows stretched (13) seeing or making friends with happy-healthy-efficient people, big men, founders, pioneers and enterprisers or listening to their voices as long as they have good self-importance, make the fire burn from within and clean up their central energy pipes.

17. Repentance may be the most effective if you have been as very devious and stubborn as don Juan Matus had been for long years

If you often repent yourself easily, such repenting yourself is little effective. If you have been devious and stubborn very much for long years, recognizing your stupidity and repenting yourself are one of the most effective. In such a case, your assemblage point will be able to move into the interior of your body. The spirit may descend to you for the first time, help you and give you supernatural power. When don Juan Matus recognized his stupidity, said thank you to his teacher, accepted his death and repented himself deeply for the first time, he could make the the fire burn from within and clean up his central energy pipe. Then, He fused himself to the emanations of the Eagle(black energy , the black apirit) at large, and glided into infinity(black energy, the black spirit ) for the first time. I think it seemed to be the biggest memorial to him. In this respect, Mr. Carlos Castaneda seemed to get so perverse that he could not have repented himself as deeply as don Juan Matus did. This may be another origin for Mr.Carlos Castaneda not to become a successor to don Juan Matus.

Repentance is like a powerful drug which is both medicine and poison for us. When you repent yourself and recognize your stupidity, you will have a body-response such as (1) feeling as if a cave opened in your abdomen and energy ascends from your abdomen (it is the evidence that the fire begins to burn from within and your central energy pipe begins to be cleaned up) (2) beginning to take a deep breath (3) stiff abdomen's turning to be fluid and relaxed. In such a case, good repentance has happened to you and your assemblage point has moved into the interior of your body so that you can shoot out your immaterial fiber or third attention to an object from your body, judge and control it. You can begin to judge accurately or realize what you imagine or recover from disease or become healthier or feel happier. Good repentance can strengthen your physical body and energy body. Such a good repentance is medicine.

To the contrary, you will not have such a comfortable body-response as that of (1)(2)(3) when you repent yourself and recognize your stupidity. In such a case, bad repentance has happened to you and your assemblage point has not moved into the interior of your body so that you can not shoot out your immaterial fiber or third attention to an object from your body and nor judge-control it. Such a bad repentance is called self-pity. You can not begin to judge accurately or can not realize what you imagine or can not recover from disease or can not become healthy or can not feel happier. Bad repentance called self-pity can weaken your physical body and energy body further. Such a bad repentance is a poison.

Good repentance is apt to happen to you when you can recognize your stupidity calmly, lively, concretely and minutely at your power-spot. Furthermore, it will happen to you easily when good complexion, rejuvenation, good bowel movement, good appetite, moderation of eating, good sleeping, good sex, soft shoulder, and subtle breath begin to happen to you little by little. If you can not repent yourself under such a condition, you are compared to the bird which falls into heavy oil sea and flounders desperately. It is bad repentance called self-pity. Unhappy-unhealthy-inefficient people are apt to do bad repentance called self-pity.

18. Nagual Julian Osario threw don Juan Matus who could not swim into the flood. He always walked along the edge of abyss. I had been nearly killed by injection in my childhood in China

We have to become modest enough to wonder if our self-importance, trust and repentance are dependable. But, usual much modesty is apt to hate danger, death or hell so that it avoids adventure, risk, desperate action. Usual much modesty is poison, so it weakens our physical bodies and energy bodies. When we become well-timed and make a dash at danger, death or hell following the tactics made by your comfortable body-response, we can often break through it. At that time, our immaterial fiber or third attention confined to our bodies can be shot out from our bodies and can judge-control danger, death or hell. In such a case, danger, death, or hell often runs away from us. Big men, founders, pioneers and enterprisers are good at this way. Whenever I go skiing, I ski on the most dangerous place without a stop.

Don Juan Matus could not swim. His teacher, Nagual Julian Osario threw him into the flood. When he accepted his death in the flood, he could calm down and enter into the peculiar inner silence. Then, his energy body was shot out of his physical body for the first time and could approach the riverbank. I think it was the second biggest memorial to him.

I was on the brink of being killed by injection by Japanese at the age of 6 in China. I have often remembered this scene. At that time, I did not fear at all, relaxed, calmed down and behaved naturally. I think behaving in such a manner made my immaterial fiber or third attention work on for me and saved my life. I slipped out a few minutes before injection. About 100 Japanese children standing around me were killed by injection. When Japanese repatriated from the northeastern region of China after the defeat of world war 2. Japanese often killed their children in China because their children were a drag on their coming back to Japan safely.

The Wheel of times says "His teacher, Julian Osario was a tubercular man who was never cured, but who lived to be perhaps 107 years old (on the earth), always walking along the edge of the abyss. Walking on the edge of the abyss meant the battle of a warrior enhanced to such a degree that every second counted. On the single moment of weakness would have thrown nagual Julian Osario into that abyss".

In this respect, Mr. Carlos Castaneda did not seem to make friends with danger or death. I think it seemed to be one of the origins for him to be unable to become a successor to don Juan Matus, too.

I like nagual Julian Osalio because he always walked along the edge of the abyss. I often imagine that I walk along the edge of the abyss in Mexico as if I were Julian Osario. I respect him because he kept on having the power to explode the energetic core of his abdomen in his central energy pipe for himself until the age of 107 on the earth in spite of his disease, could explode it and could fuse with the universe at last without losing his consciousness. I sometimes wonder if I can imitate him. If I become weak, careless or proud from now on, I will die of disease such as cancer and heart disease or die of a accident on the earth although I can already have ventured out to the universe.

The energy body of an old smallish virile lean woman like a female hawk sometimes has visited me to Japan all the way from U.S.A since the Tensegrity in the summer of 1998 in U.S.A which I attended. Her energy body visited me at a motel near the hall of Tensegrity. I have not met her physical body yet. But, I respect her, too, because she has kept on making big efforts to fight against Old Age called the last enemy of a man of knowledge. I can feel she is doing so privately.

19. The right way of walking is a good weapon to fight against Old Age. Then, the sky just above the horizon is the secret door of another world

While walking in the right way of walking, the sky just above the horizon seems like a female womb or the secret door of another world or the body of opposite sex. Then, you can enter into or touch it. It seems like a rope ladder which a helicopter hangs, too. If you can catch it, you will be lifted to the universe. It seems like a bending intent of the earth or of a star, too. You can catch it, make it straight upward and make it shoot out or return to the universe from the horizon.

Furthermore, the sky just above the horizon can erase your stickiness and temper your energy body. While keeping on walking in such way for 3-4 hours without rest or soft drink, I seldom become tired. I think the right way of walking can make you healthier and stronger. It seems to multiply the ability for you to move in your dream and to change your dream freely. There are many kinds of devils such as a mud shadow in the inner space or on the surface of earth whose size is half an inch-the same size of France. They live anywhere. They are apt to stick to sleeping human being and absorb the energy of human being. When I notice them and get angry, they are apt to run away obediently. I think the right way of walking can multiply the ability to shut out such devils from your body.

It is more effective for you that you manage to make your eyes and the way of walking have happy lucky healthy young feeling as much as possible while walking. In addition, you had better sometimes talk to yourself and something (someone, animal, tree, flower, cloud, sun, star or moon) with the feeling of abandon, largess and humor while walking. If you can begin to practice changing your bad feeling to good feeling, you can become aware for the first time that you have kept on having the bad feeling of your eyes, of your thoughts, of your voices and of your behaviors for long years. You can begin to throw away your bad feeling for the first time just after you can begin to aware that you have kept on having bad feeling for long years. Most of us have been confined to only one or two feelings for long years. Most of us have had much stickiness in eyes, behind eyes or around eyes which has made most of us confined to one or two feeling for long years.

Eyes are connected with internal organs through energy channels. If we have the eyes of bad feeling, we have to have weak unhealthy internal organ. If we have weak unhealthy internal organ, we have to have the eyes of bad feeling, too. When you can begin to throw away the bad feeling which you have cherished unconsciously for long years, I think you must feel as if you cut the trunk of big snake or big chain. Then, you feel that big vortex will happen to the central energy pipe near your weak unhealthy internal organ and feel that your eyes will become clear.

I often make the energy of my hand and of my elbow catch or break through the sky just above the horizon while walking, too. This is the good way to make hand and elbow sensitive.

I feel don Juan Matus and don Genaro ate four mouthfuls of food at one time and walked miles and miles everyday on the earth. They seemed to eat in more moderation and walked more than Mr. Carlos Castaneda and me. So, I can see their legs and waists of their energy bodies are much stronger than those of Mr. Carlos Castaneda and me. I have taken for a walk for an hour everyday since 20 years ago and have walked for 3-4 hours once a week or once a month since 10 years ago whenever I feel stuck or irritated. I am 59 year old Japanese and have grown 10-25 years old younger. But, don Juan Matus looked younger on the earth than his son who was a career soldier in his mid-sixties. Growing at least 10-20 years old younger is the evidence to make the fire burn from within.

I think that eating so and walking so everyday can make you feel happier, make the fire burn from within your abdomen and can make you grow much younger. I think you will never die of cancer as long as you do so at least a few times a week. I think it is a good weapon to fight against the last enemy called Old Age. I owe much gratitude to Mr.Carlos Castaneda because he was taught about it by don Juan Matus and taught it to me through his books.

There are hundreds of ways to temper our bodies and energy bodies. If we begin to know many ways, we are apt to rove from one way to another, skip and end up practicing no way. It can be compared to roving from one woman (or one man) to another woman (or another man) and ending up marrying no woman(or no man) or marrying a bad woman(or a bad man). So, those who know many ways are apt to die of cancer, of heart disease or of high blood pressure or be unable to live long. The teacher who teaches how to temper physical body and energy body is apt to have the same inclination. Knowing is not practicing. I am careful not to become so because I know many ways. Only knowing eating four mouthfuls of food at one time and walking in the right way everyday for long years is much effective for us than knowing many ways, skipping and ending up practicing no way. So, I have written about it again here.

20. Reading many books can weaken your body and heart. Be careful not to be influenced by the bad feeling (?) of Mr. Carlos Castaneda

I have read about 2000 books about psychic world, religion, body exercise and another world for 30 years. But, most books have been useless for me after all. I think I have wasted time on reading many books and it has weakened my physical body and energy body fairly.

I can have noticed one of the devils which has stuck to me or stolen into me or been floating above me. It is the devil that has prodded me to do something hurriedly or has made me endeavor to do something busily or has made me trapped in somewhere. This devil has made me a mouse in a rotating ring. This devil has made me read many books, too. This devil has made me a slavery of book. In such a case, good body-response has never happened to me and I feel gloomy and depressing. Then, my immaterial fiber or third attention is confined to my body and can not work on for me because good body-response has never happened to you. As a result, this devil has made me have undependable self-importance, undependable trust and self-pity. This devil has made my eyes severe or sticky or irritated or restless. I am confined to an illusion. I can not realize what I imagine or think of. You have been stolen into by the same type of devil as that of my devil, haven't you? Have you been like a mouse in a rotating ring in a certain area such as book, opposite sex, money, post, fame, faith, plan, religion, drug or alcohol?

For me, this devil seems as if it were tenacious sticky snake whose color is transparent and gray because it has lived in my bones and my body for about 40 years. I have begun to fight against it since a year ago. I have tried to make more beautiful stronger different fire burn from within my body strengthening the function of my radiator (white energy of my lung). I will burn this devil if this devil has kept on staying and interfered in me. In these days, I buy and read a book only when I can feel good body-response (for example, I can feel relieved or relaxed or light) glancing at a book without opening a book in a bookstore. Furthermore, I have tried to change my eyes for better when I can notice I have bad eyes again. It is because we can not beckon the spirit as long as we have bad eyes. Bad eyes can beckon not the spirit but devils. Bad eyes can beckon not good opposite sex but bad opposite sex, too. Good eyes which has the feeling of abandon, largesse, humor can beckon the spirit and good opposite sexes.

So, instead of reading many books, you had better concentrate on your breath almost all day for 3 weeks at a power-spot to stop your breath automatically, beckon an ally and the spirit, stare at something with your eyebrows broadened, fast, run the risk at your peril and walk in the right way. They will teach you more than reading many books. Concentrating on your breath almost all day for 3 weeks to stop your breath automatically is more effective to research the universe, another world and psychic world than reading 1000 books. Without it, you can not understand them at all.

Mr. Carlos Castaneda's 12 books are almost enough. But, they do not seem to make a point of stopping your breath automatically, circulating your second attention in your physical body, burning the fire from within concretely, cleaning up your central energy pipe, making the beautiful strong energetic core of abdomen, flexible and firm abdomen, good spine, the secret of physiognomy, good complexion, rejuvenation, fasting, influence of other people and of devils, cutting the pipe of floating devil above your head, good relationship with opposite sex, dependable self-importance, good repentance, imagining powerful men such as Christ, or absorbing the power of various voices and of various flights. So, I have added them to my book. I think Mr. Carlos Castaneda would have never died of liver cancer if he had practiced them. Needless to say, not smoking is essential to research the universe and another world.

Furthermore, you had better be careful not to be influenced by the bad feeling (the bad mood) of Mr. Carlos Castaneda when you read his books many times. Mr.Carlos Castaneda said "In fact, I had never thanked anyone, ever" and Don Juan Matus said to Mr.Carlos Castaneda "Jorge Compos and Lucas Coronado are two ends of an axis. That axis is you, at one end a ruthless, shameless, crass mercenary who take care of himself; hideous, but indestructible. At the other end a super-sensitive, tormented artist, weak and vulnerable. That should have been the map of your life" in the book with title-The Active Side of Infinity.

In most cases, a bad feeling such as that of a ruthless, shameless, crass mercenary, and of a super-sensitive, tormented artist is brought about by the devil which has the same bad feelings. Such a devil sticks to or steals into someone so that it brings about the same bad feeling to someone and tortures-weakens someone. I felt I had become fairly timid since 2 years ago, so a year ago I could find the black brown timid devil had stolen into and lived in my body. If you can notice new different bad feeling, you had better check your body and shut out the devil which has the same bad feeling from your body.

21. You had better imagine Christ and Paul who did not fear the death and devoted themselves to the spirit, and can move your assemblage point deeply

In this respect, I recommend that you had better read New Testament many times and catch the feeling of Christ and of Paul who did not fear the death and devoted themselves to the spirit. Christ was young, walked enough everyday and never made ** with an opposite sex?, so he was very energetic and comported himself with confidence. Most of us can not imitate him because most of us have neither walked enough everyday nor saved sex energy at all. I think Christ could beckon the spirit easily and handle it freely. Christ could shoot out his strong immaterial fiber or third attention to an object, too. So, he could do many marvelous acts. I feel the energy body (the consciousness) of Christ has been living in the universe and watching human-race.

I visited Jerusalem about 20 years ago. I felt as if I came back to my hometown when our bus was approaching Jerusalem just before sunset. I felt relieved and relaxed. My abdomen became warm. When I remembered the stone recently where Christ sat down all night at the last night on the earth, I saw that strong black energy suddenly overflowed into all over the world from this stone and the inner space turned to be red. I saw the inside of the Scriptures was burning, too. I can have understood that Christ said "I have come to set fire to the earth " (Revised English Bible). I can believe that Christ said "I will come and stay where a few men gather in my name".

If we read about Christ many times and imagine as if we were Christ in Israel 2000 years ago walking enough everyday and saving our sex energy as possible, our assemblage points will easily move into the same interior of our physical bodies as that of Christ so that we can do the same acts as those of Christ did.

In addition, I recommend that you had better read LES PAGES IMMORTELLS DE NAPOLEON and imagine Napoleon's successes and ruin because he had had the fire within his body and could have shot out his immaterial fiber or third attention by the war against Russia. He had had the attribute of a warrior which are control, discipline, forbearance, timing and will (immaterial fiber and third attention) until the war against Russia. He had made friends with danger and death. I think he seemed to have known body-response such as a voice without a voice and to have known overwhelming premonition which is the impulse of strong healthy kidney's black energy. Following such a body-response, he seemed to have made many victories under a difficult condition by the war against Russia.

I think an origin of the Napoleon's downfall seemed to be a bad relationship with opposite sex. It seemed to have deprived him of joy, light, sweetness and peace and seemed to have weakened his abdomen, his immaterial fiber and third attention. I feel Napoleon had thirsted for joy, light spring breeze's feeling, sweetness and peace at the bottom of his heart for long years. He seemed to have become like a machine without lubrication at last. He might have become at least the emperor of all Europe if he had married such a woman as she could satisfy his thirstiness. Our immaterial fibers and third attention are very strong and very naive. They can be compared to a young virgin who has missiles warhead. They are very shy and very fierce. Without joy, light spring breeze's feeling, sweetness or peace, they will become almost dead or useless at last. Or, they will hide from us soon if we handle them without joy, light spring breeze's feeling, sweetness or peace.

So, you had better make every effort not to throw away such a good feeling (in your eyes, voice, behavior, and thought) even though you are under a difficult condition. Don't get perverse. I repeat that you can begin to get back such a good feeling in 2-3 months if you begin to practice Part 1 of my book everyday as possible. As a result, you can begin to burn the strong beautiful fire within your body, begin to have good complexion, begin to have flexible and firm abdomen and waist, and begin to grow younger. Don't depend upon other people. Get up for yourself if you have not been rotten to the core or you want not to die of cancer or heart disease at last.

You will surely be able to meet an ally (or the spirit) and venture out to the universe sooner or later if you read what I have written, the pages of meeting an ally (or the spirit) and the pages of energy body's flight in Mr.Carlos Castaneda's books, Ancient Egyptian Pyramid Text, The Emerald-Tablet of Thoth-The-Atlantean and New Testament as many as possible and imagine as lively as possible as if you met an ally (or the spirit) and ventured out to the universe. If you are ready for death that may be caused by an ally (or the spirit), I recommend that you will try.

I think being killed by an ally, the spirit and the universe is manlier than being killed by cancer or heart disease. Ironically, I have sometimes become on the brink of being killed by an ally, the spirit and universe, but I have survived. Don Juan Matus said "We can win if we can make our enemies empty". But, in such a case, I was attacked by emptiness when I thought I had won. Anyway, I think an ally, the spirit and the universe like the human being who is ready for death and dares to approach them. You had better not fear them as Mr.Carlos Castaneda did.

22. You had better enter into another world through voice or sound. Absorb the feeling of various flights

Lastly, I recommend to you that you will be able to open the gate of another world or of the universe by catching the energy of sounds or of voices.

You had better study the difference between the voice of unhealthy-unhappy-inefficient people and the voice of healthy-happy-efficient people. You had better study the difference between the voice or music which can beckon the spirit and the voice or music which can not beckon the spirit. I recommend you will listen to the music disc of Ventures as many times as possible because Ventures can emit the feeling of abandon, of largess, and of humor which the spirit likes very much. In addition, you had better study the difference between the voice which careless or proud people utter and the voice which careful or alert people utter.

Furthermore, you had better listen to many various ethnic musics and foreign languages. You had better be able to see the colors of ethnic musics and of foreign languages and notice the smells, touch's senses, temperature of ethnic musics and of foreign languages. You had better be able to classify the energies of voices and of sounds into the feeling of spring, the feeling of summer, the feeling of autumn and the feeling of winter. You had better be able to find what type of an ally, of the spirit, of a devil and of an angel these ethnic musics and foreign languages are apt to beckon. You had better imagine the fates, prosperity and tragedy which the feelings of these ethnic musics and of foreign languages have brought about to the races who have sung such ethnic musics and spoken in such languages. For example, you had better listen to Israeli fork songs and imagine the ups and downs of Israel.

When you can catch the energy of voice or of sound as if it were a substance, you can enter into another world and the universe through the energy of voice or of sound. For example, innumerable places of the universe have been exploding as if the universe beaten innumerable bass drums. If you can listen to a roll of the universe's drums, you will waver at the beginning and be able to temper yourself by its shock as if you were an iron. Its shock seems to deprive you of weakness, vagueness, timidity and indecision. Its shock can make you strengthen to become a strong psychic astronaut.

★ Eagle is like a slow heavy ball, but is stronger than falcon and hawk

A year ago when a noble eagle which was white with blue splashes descended to me again from the far distant cold universe, I said to him "You have descended to such a dirty human being as me all the way from the far distant universe. Thank you". When I remember the feeling of the white eagle's flight, I feel much relieved and feel that the gate of the universe has opened widely.

There are many ways to fly in the universe. So, you had better absorb the feelings of various flights. You had better study the feelings of various birds' flights, of various bullets' flights, of various cannon-shells' flights, of various balls' flights, of various missiles' flight, of various planes' flights, of various spaceships' flights and so on. For example, eagle is not so fast as falcon or hawk. The feeling of eagle's flight is slow and heavy. But, it has the strong power to break through anything and to deprive enemies of their power, resistance. It has the feeling not of a fastball but of a slow heavy ball. A batter can hit a fastball easily, but can not hit a slow heavy ball easily. I think eagle has more black energy than falcon or hawk. A pitcher of slow heavy ball has more flexible and firmer abdomen and waist than a pitcher of fastball has. He emits stronger and more beautiful energy from his abdomen and waist than a pitcher of fastball does. I think we have to fly into the universe as eagle if we vanish our physical bodies and do not return to the surface of the earth forever. I feel a plane of high fare has more feeling of eagle and of slow heavy ball than a plane of low fare has although the type of planes is the same.

23. Don't underestimate the death defier because she has special strong calm energy which can move within the universe freely

The death defier (known to the sorcerer's lineage of don Juan Matus as the tenant) has calm, immense, lukewarm energy whose color is the blend of white, yellow, transparence and red. I met her 3 days ago in the universe. Then, Julian Osario's energy body turned to be more powerful and its color changed from the blend of white and gray to the rustling blend of blue, transparency and black. Somehow, he seemed to gain more freedom in the universe. Next night, her energy body seemed to enter into my bed and stay there. Don Juan Matus hated her because she was lechery. He lost his virginity because he made ** with her. But, I think she has the peculiar feeling and power. They are worthy for you to study. Don't underestimate her. The gate to enter into the death defier's world is the feeling of Ms. Carol Tiggs because Ms.Carol Tiggs once fused with the death defier. When you see Ms.Carol Tiggs, you had better not forget the feeling of Ms.Carol Tiggs.

The death defier has strong calm transparent energy, too. When I concentrated my attention on her strong calm transparent energy last night, my sex organ was suddenly vanished to emptiness by it.

Don Juan Matus and Julian Osario did not agree to my attending the Tensegrity workshops in the summer of 1998 in U.S.A. Whenever I glanced at the sky just above the horizon taking for a walk and wondering if I attended it, a big flash lightened just above the horizon. The interplay of energy on the horizon happened to me as the book with the title-The Active Side of Infinity says, so I attended the Tensegrity workshops in the summer of 1998 in U.S.A. I saw Ms.Carol Tiggs there and I could meet the death defier 3 days ago through Ms.Carol Tigge's feeling. I have accomplished the meaning of my attending it.

24. My next subject is to research the secret of gravity which is black energy

I have been researching the secret of gravity since a year ago. I think the core of gravity is black energy. Black energy is connected with some element of salt. I think black energy is connected with the sea's layer which is 800-3000 m deep, too. Whales dive to this deep sea's layer and can transmit their voices to one after another within this deep sea's layer at the speed of 1000 km a second. When my energy body crossed over the Pacific under water within 1-2 seconds, it seemed to make a sudden dart for the continent of America from Japan within the sea's layer which is 800-3000 m deep.

Black energy parts from other energy and substance, and condenses. After condensation, some of black energy rushes to where it wants to approach. Black energy duplicates condensation and shooting each other. Black energy makes bones in physical body of human being. Black energy forms the shape of other energy or of substance and binds it together. I think transparent energy helps black energy because it invades into black energy and engulfs it .If all black energy and all transparent energy part from other energy or substance, other energy or substance will be exploded to pieces or melted.

Yellow energy is connected with some element of sugar. If yellow energy resolves and devours the black energy in other energy or substance, other energy or substance will be exploded to pieces or melted. I think black energy is the core of our lives. If a machine is invented which can resolve and devour the black energy, it will be used as a weapon or medical treatment.

Furthermore, black energy teaches us an accurate information as a silent voice when some of black energy rushes from our physical bodies to where it wants to approach. I have often seen that the tip of flying thought or of flying voice is an energy ball whose core is black energy. I think we can feel the most satisfied and happiest when some of our black energy can rush to where it wants to approach. If we often prevent some of our black energy from rushing to where it wants to approach, we will feel irritated, depressed or stuck and will be rotten to the core at last. I can awake I have often done so whenever I remember my life in detail. Enlightenment of Buddhism is to eliminate such irritation, depression and repression.

According to modern physics about the earth, the origin of magnetic force of the earth is the outer core of the earth that is made of fluid alloy of iron and of nickel. The outer core of the earth is 2200 km thick. The core of the earth is made of solid alloy of iron and of nickel which is 1300 km in radius. Its temperature is 4000 c'. I think the red energy of the earth and of the universe descend to the black energy of the core of the earth. The red energy and the black energy are fused within the core of the earth so that they can produce the yellow energy within the core of the earth. The surface of the earth is 35 km thick. The mantle below the surface is 2900 km thick. I can see that the surface of the earth is made of rock whose energetic color is green and the mantle is burning. Whenever my immaterial fiber or third attention enters into the fluid outer core of the earth, I feel the same feeling as that of my head's top's nectar. I can feel sweet, cool, transparent and fluid. I feel relieved and sacred.

I think iron is the origin of gravity and of magnetic force. Modern astronomers say that the core of Milky Way is made of the element of iron that is in super high temperatures, too. Furthermore, I think that iron is emitting not only negative ion which make us healthy but also something sacred which can beckon the spirit and open the gate of universe. In this respect, the granite of Ancient Egyptian Pyramid has contained much melted iron and emits much negative ion. According to Ancient Egyptian Pyramid Text, Akhuses live in the most sacred place of the universe and have tools of iron that can open the mouth of human being's energy body who can enter into the most sacred place of the universe. The energy body can enter into the interior of the universe further after his mouth is opened by the iron tool of Akhus. In connection with the secret of gravity, I will research what iron emits, too.

25. Regrettably, the more we can recognize our stupidity deeply, the more we can become healthier and efficient

Whenever I remember the events of my life in detail, I can recognize that I can seldom have shot out my immaterial fiber or third attention to an object. To my great regret, I am compelled to recognize that I have been stupid and a blockhead for long years. I have been so stubborn that I have almost ignored the spirit (or an ally) and my body-response. I have been apt to indulge in bad self-importance, undependable trust and self-pity which have weakened me for long years.

I have often dealt with other people vaguely, too. I have often been irresponsible for a result. In such a case, my immaterial fiber or third attention is not used and is confined to my body. Such a vague behavior has weakened my immaterial fiber or third attention.

Furthermore, I am surprised to find that I have almost made friends or acquaintances with same people as me.

When most big men, founders, pioneers or enterprisers reach the pinnacle of success, they have begun to be unable to handle their immaterial fibers or third attention and begun to have bad self-importance, undependable trust and self-pity, too. Most of them have ruined 3-10 later after they had become proud or careless.

Foolishly, I had smoked 2 packs of tobacco everyday until 4 years ago. My head was affected by the smoke of tobacco. If you read my book as many times as possible and remember your life lively at least 100 times, you will surely recognize that you have been almost stupid for long years, too.

For long years, I have aimlessly got angry at environmental pollution such as dirty air, water, river and sea, and at tree's having been cut down indiscriminately. I have indulged in such an aimless anger for long year. When you indulge in an aimless anger for long time, your immaterial fiber or third attention is not used and confined to your body so that it will easily become almost dead. If you get angry, you have to improve your surroundings by using your immaterial fiber or third attention. If you can not do so, you have to try to stop getting angry or have to try to run away or have to be indifferent by all means. Before you decide to fight (or how to fight) or run away or be indifferent, we have to be vague. But, you indulge in vagueness for long time, you will be rotten to the core.

In addition, I had hated several big vinyl houses in front of my house for about 20 years because the vegetables in these vinyl houses have the same feeling of melancholic. I could notice that I had indulged in an aimless anger and absorbed the same feeling of melancholic from these vegetables unconsciously for long years. A week ago when I walked beside these vinyl houses, I talked to the vegetables in these vinyl houses. By using my third attention, I said to these vegetables "Please, excuse human beings who will eat you soon. Don't get perverse as long as you live on the earth. Please, grow and live lively even though you can have short lives on the earth". When such a message could reach the vegetables in the vinyl house by me, beautiful transparent flash suddenly lightened in the vinyl house by me and the vegetables turned to be lively. Then, I could feel relieved and joyful.

Strangely, I can become relieved, relaxed, and can feel happier, healthier, more efficient whenever I can have recognized my stupidity and the bad influence of other people, of environmental pollution and of our surroundings deeply. The more we can recognize our stupidity deeply, the more we can have good health and supernatural power.

So, I recommend to you that you will remember your life in detail as many times as possible reading my book as many times as possible.

26. Say thank you to Mr. Carlos Castaneda, publishing companies, earnest readers, allies, the spirits, many kind people and my wife

Now, I say thank you to the late Mr.Carlos Castaneda and the publishing companies that have published his books. Owing to his books, I can have proceeded more to a man of knowledge or a path of a warrior. When I read his last three books with the title-Magical Passes, The Wheel of Time and The Active Side of Infinity, I felt as if he knew that he would die of liver cancer in 1998. He seemed to have written before his death whatever he had been taught by don Juan Matus because he seemed to know that he did not have the ability to become the successor to don Juan Matus. Mr. Carlos Castaneda hoped someone of those who read his books will become a successor to don Juan Matus.

According to some internet, he seemed to have earned about 20 million dollars to write his best seller books. I feel sorry that he died of liver cancer at the age of 72 (?) in 1998. I wonder why he did not pay his second attention to the energy body of don Genaro who is floating in the universe. Don Genaro had loved and taught Mr. Carlos Castaneda very much before the departure to the universe. Don Genaro has much beautiful transparent green energy like light spring breeze that can cure liver disease easily. In addition, Mr. Carlos Castaneda might not have practiced what don Juan Matus taught him earnestly everyday.

But, I think Mr. Carlos Castaneda accomplished the feat to introduce the ancient Inca-knowledge (how to move our assemblage points freely, how to become healthy-happy-efficient, how to bring up our immaterial fibers or third attention, the hidden supernatural power of human being, how to beckon the spirit, how to become a psychic astronaut, and how to fuse with the universe without losing consciousness and live there for 2 billion years? as an inorganic being (phenix). He sent another new bible to the world.

When I begun to read his books 7 years ago, I had no confidence to write in more detail than his books at all. Reviewing his books, I think now I can have added my different messages to his books. It takes me 6 years to multiply the contents of his books by about 30%. I hope someone will understand what I have written and multiply the contents of what I have written. Furthermore, I hope someone will be able to become a psychic astronaut and write a book as to how to become a psychic astronaut referring to what I have written, to his books, to Emerald-Tablets of Thoth, to Ancient Egyptian Pyramid Text, to Yoga Sutra and to Cabala. I feel much pleased even though you practice some part of what I have written only to become healthy-happy-efficientor or only grow younger at your peril.

Finally, I would like to express to the earnest readers my deepest gratitude for finishing reading what I have written in bad English. The spirits bless you !

Furthermore, I say thank you to many inorganic allies, many spirits who have taught and guarded me in spite of my stupidity and stubbornness, many people who have shown me their kindness in my life and my wife.

The End

# *About the Author*

Hiroyuki Nishigaki. Japanese born in 1941. Author of four books in Japanese-Enlightenment of Buddha, How to Attain Silent Knowledge, How to Concentrate on Your Breath and Stop it Automatically. A psychic astronaut since 3 years ago. From Osaka City University.

# *Bibliography*

_A Separate Reality by Carlos Castaneda

_Enlightenment of Buddha(in Japanese) by Hiroyuki Nishigaki

_Executive ESP by Douglas Dean

_How to Attain Silent Knowledge (in Japanese) by Hiroyuki Nishigaki

_How to Concentrate on Your Breath and Stop it Automatically (in Japanese) by Hiroyuki Nishigaki

_Journey to Ixtlan by Carlos Castaneda

_Kabbala by Muriel. Doreal

_Keeper of Genesis by Robert Bauval and Graham Hancock

_LES PAGES IMMORTELLS DE NAPOLEON

_Magical Passes by Carlos Castaneda

_New Cosmos Series (in Japanese)

_Tales of Power by Carlos Castaneda

_Temper Your Body as Steel by Fan Ke Ping

_The Active Side of Infinity by Carlos Castaneda

_The Art of Dreaming by Carlos Castaneda

_The Eagle's Gift by Carlos Castaneda

_The Emerald-Tablets of Thoth-The-Atlantean by Muriel. Doreal

_The Fire from Within by Carlos Castaneda

_The Medicine of Ancient Chinese Yellow Emperor by Takeo Kosoto and Toshiyuki Hamada(in Japanese)

_The Miracle of Mind Dynamics by Joseph Murphy

_The Original Sources of Buddha by Humio Mashutani (in Japanese)

_The Power of Silence by Carlos Castaneda

_The Revised English Bible(Oxford Cambridge)

_The Structure of The Earth by Youzou Hamano (in Japanese)

_The Second Ring of Power by Carlos Castaneda

_The Teachings of Don Juan by Carlos Castaneda

_The Wheel of Time by Carlos Castaneda

_Urban Shaman by Serge Kahili King

_Yoga Sutra by Turuzi Sahota (in Japanese)

Printed in the United States
56964LVS00004B/212

9 780595 001330